Linda –
Cheers to great
neighbors!
Lisa
3/07/20

50/50

CRAWLING ACROSS BROKEN GLASS

How One Woman Fought Gender Discrimination, Beat the Odds, and Won

‖‖

LISA SHIPLEY

‖‖

ISBN 978-0-692249-70-3

Printed in the United States of America.

To my son Daniel, who asked me the question that got me to tell this story nine months after the trial was over: "Mom—is this going to be another one of those projects/ideas that you really want to do that never happens because you're just too busy?" Thank you Daniel for helping me to finish something that was so very personal and important to me.

Love, Mom

CONTENTS

"*They made Lisa fight and scrape and crawl on hands and knees across glass to win this case. They tried everything they could to win this claim, to demean her, to bankrupt her. And she prevailed because she was right.*"

—David B. Ritter
Neal Gerber & Eisenberg, LLP

INTRODUCTION

My name is Lisa Shipley.

Like many career-oriented women, when I entered the workforce I dreamed of breaking the proverbial glass ceiling by diligently working hard and excelling in my chosen profession. By all standards, I did just that. Through hard work and outstanding performance, I became one of the five highest-ranking sales executives—and the only woman—at Hypercom, a publicly traded, global corporation well-known for being highly dominated by men. Because of my work ethic and achievements I was well regarded and valued by six different male presidents/CEOs, respected by my colleagues and sales team, and recognized as a leader within my industry—even bestowed with honors. For 12 straight years I remained loyal to my employer in an industry commonly known for job-hopping—even among the most senior positions.

So what went wrong?

I hit an unexpected barrier—a gender-biased cultural barrier.

My whole world changed when Philippe Tartavull, a Hypercom board member who had previously been president of Oberthur Card Systems North and Central America, a French company, was named president and CEO of Hypercom. Nearly ten months later, after I had closed the biggest quarter in North American sales the company had ever seen, I walked away from a corporation for which I had lucratively performed for more than 12 years. Under this man's discriminatory leadership, I could no longer endure the pure hell he put me through for ten strenuous months. His gender bias was exceptionally apparent, highly abusive, and increased in intensity over time.

After years of loyalty, I felt the only way to survive professionally was to accept a similar position with another company in the same industry. I had no intention of doing anything beyond removing myself from this intolerable situation so that I could move on with my career and my life. But after negotiating for months with this man to approve paying me commissions that I had rightfully earned during my final quarter with the company, commissions that he had willingly paid to those who had worked under me, he flatly refused. That was the last straw.

So, despite the stigma that is often thrust upon a woman who claims gender discrimination, in January 2009, one year after resigning and fighting for what was rightfully mine, I filed a gender discrimination lawsuit. Little did I realize that filing that lawsuit would be the beginning of a long and arduous four-year ordeal, filled with calculated delays by Hypercom (the defendant) escalating legal costs, leveling malicious accusations, and creating enormous emotional stress for me.

When the case finally went to trial, there were five long days of testimony. Hypercom's lawyers tried everything they could to manipulate facts, discredit my claims, and demean me—to bankrupt me. I cried repeatedly on the witness stand. Each day was gut wrenching.

So, was it worth it?

As I take you behind the scenes and share my whole story, you be the judge. And as you do, please keep in mind that my sole passion in sharing this story with you is not to discourage you in pursuit of your ambitions and dreams, it is to convey to you the challenges that women continue to face—even more now as we endeavor to climb the ladder of success in a global and culturally diverse business world. For purposes of reader clarification, a minimal amount of editing was made to the trial transcripts—no material facts were changed. Everything in this book really happened.

I continue to believe that with perseverance, integrity, and hard work we can still achieve our ultimate dreams, yet I also believe we must have a keen awareness of the potential bias and pitfalls that unfortunately still exist.

Here is my story.

- 1 -

BALANCING ACT

You may be wondering—just who is Lisa Shipley? Well, I'm typical of my generation—probably not much different from many other women. I am a woman who hoped to find a career that would motivate me to go to work each day until I would one day marry and have children.

Perhaps the one thing that was unique for me, however, was that I grew up as one of nine children. It was crazy, but we had a lot of fun. We fought all the time and were creative in the way we fought. As an example, our family raised Alaskan malamute dogs. These dogs loved peanut butter, so if any one of us "ratted" on the other to Mom or Dad, as soon as our parents left we'd all pin down the sibling who ratted and smear peanut butter on his or her face. Then we let the dogs in and the licking would begin. As kids we thought it was hysterical, but when we weren't tantalizing them with peanut butter the dogs were gentle and wonderful companions.

Despite these childish antics, we cared deeply for one another. We were and still are absolutely inseparable. Even today as adults we get together every chance we can; we even vacation together and always have so much fun that people who meet us along the way have actually asked jokingly if we'd adopt them. We have a bond that I've rarely seen in other families. I have to say "kudos" to my mom and dad. Even without having the money they needed to make ends meet, they made do and did a darn good job of it. And the fact is that with nine of us, we had to be creative to get attention, which I think resulted in us all being very competitive and led us to all being successful in our adult lives.

By the time I was 18 I knew that I wanted to go to college, and I enrolled at Western Illinois University for two years. I got a job as an assistant dorm director, which paid for my room and board my second year. When summer came I took my vacation in Virginia, visiting a cousin. While there, I met and fell for a boy. So after vacation I packed all my possessions into a Honda Hatchback and drove back to Virginia. I took a job as a waitress and tended bar to cover living expenses and lived like a pauper. When I'd saved enough money, I enrolled at Old Dominion University and resumed taking courses. It took seven years for me to finally get a degree. In the meantime, I broke up with that early summer romance and met a new love my final year of college. I married him, and we had three children together, our twins first. It's funny, but when I got married I actually thought I would only work as long as it took me to get pregnant. But due to fertility issues it took longer than I thought it would, during which time I got a taste of some small success in the business world. After the birth of the twins I soon realized how hard it was to be a stay-at-home mom and begged to go back to work.

Unfortunately, when the twins were three and the youngest was one, I separated from my husband—eventually divorcing him. Knowing I would now likely be the primary source of support for my children, my number one driving force was finding employment.

I had taken a low-paying job as a temporary clerk at a bank but also continued to work as a waitress to make ends meet. At the time I don't think I ever intended to stay in banking, but I was delighted when in less than a year the bank promoted me to a supervisory position. Two years later I was named assistant vice president.

I often muse about how interesting it is that life puts us right where we belong and we don't even realize it at the time. While I may not have intentionally planned to grow my career in banking, it soon became apparent that I was exactly where I was meant to be when along with the vice president promotion came an interesting challenge—one that I could never have planned.

A brand-new technology had been introduced to our industry that would allow stores and banks to process credit card sales electronically. With my promotion, I was put in charge of the group that would be responsible for introducing this new product to our customers. I was captivated by this new technology, and the thought of how it could impact our entire industry and our customers energized me. Then amazingly at age 33 and a single mother of three I was asked by the bank to become president of one of its companies—Terminal Management Systems Company (TMS), a technology-related company dealing with the new electronic processing equipment. As president, I would be responsible for the sales and marketing of equipment that made electronic sales possible for banks and retailers.

Outwardly I appeared to be a huge success, and inwardly I saw myself as Wonder Woman, yet I was trying desperately to balance the mounds of new responsibilities that were changing daily. I had set the bar so high that I never allowed myself to say "no" to anything anyone asked of me— not at work and not at home. I was flying around the country every week for business while I was also volunteering at the kids' school. Most days my life was absolutely hectic, and my colleagues and friends had no idea of the stress, anxiety, and exhaustion I lived with every day. They saw this perfect woman who was able to juggle it all. And I continued to do everything I could to keep that image alive.

||||||||||

Being president of TMS put me in a position where I learned a whole new world—the world of POS, or point of sale. At the time when merchants made a credit card sale they used a bulky machine that we called a "knuckle buster." You placed the credit card in a groove, laid a three-part form on top of that, and then pulled a lever down to create an imprint of the card. Remember those machines?

The new technology transformed and simplified that laborious procedure into a simple swipe of the credit card. But understanding all that was needed to support that process was not so simple and I had a lot to learn—which I did. Little did I realize at the time, however, that this new knowledge would lead to a major turning point in my career.

The bank decided to sell TMS to a global, publicly traded firm, which at the time was the largest credit card processor in the country. When the twins were five and my youngest was three, the job took me to Atlanta— away from Virginia and from the children's dad. This added even more pressure on me to be successful. The hard work paid off though and soon I became a full vice president. After six months in Atlanta I began to feel it just wasn't a good fit. At the bank I had sold a lot of credit card equipment, and I'd heard how lucrative selling this equipment could be and realized how much more money I could make if I pursued sales. So I went to work for Hypercom, a company that designed, manufactured, and sold credit card processing equipment, including the terminals with the new card swiping technology. I was hired to be the sales director for a 10- to 12-state area of the southeastern United States. I would now be in charge of selling electronic credit card processing machines to banks and other companies that processed credit card transactions. All the knowledge I had acquired to perform my previous support role would now be used to introduce prospective customers to Hypercom's equipment—and of course to sell it to them.

One bank in Memphis, Tennessee, although small, bought large quantities of credit card processing machines from Hypercom's biggest competitor. I was sent to call on this bank to see if I could capture some of its business. Over a period of time, not only did I capture *some* of the business, but I also ended up securing an $11 million order. For that one achievement I was publicly recognized at a sales dinner and presented with an impressively large eagle statue. On the base was engraved, "The Eleven Million Dollar Lady." This one account became so important that at one point I had a corporate apartment in Memphis where I spent three to four days a week just so I could manage the account. With a later $28 million order, this one small bank became Hypercom's largest account.

Although the industry was known to be male dominated, here I was, the company's only senior saleswoman. But I never thought a lot about being female versus male. I was always treated as "one of the guys" by my peers, and I was fine with that. And when I became the company's number one salesperson I felt that I was truly judged solely on my performance and how I treated others. I simply felt appreciated and was proud that I had earned the respect of my peers and superiors.

My hard work and diligence did not go without recognition from senior management either. Eventually I was asked to take over as president of one of Hypercom's companies called Horizon Group. This company had 300 employees and supported the hardware for credit card transaction machines. It was a major promotion and one I felt honored to be given. But it was primarily a people-managing role and didn't involve direct sales, and as time passed I really missed being in sales. Apparently Hypercom missed me in sales too because one year later the company pulled me back into its side of the business and offered me the position of senior vice president of North American sales.

It was an offer I readily accepted.

This promotion made me the highest-ranking female employee in the company and the only female executive. I was now one of a global group of five senior vice presidents; the other four were men who served the international markets of Europe, Asia, South America, and Mexico and the Caribbean. Although serving different markets, our primary responsibilities were the same—with one exception. Because North America was somewhat unique in its customer mix, I was given the additional responsibility of selling credit card equipment to a group of prospective customers known as independent sales organizations (ISOs), as well as to our regular customer base. This was a new concept that had never been tried before, and like anything new, the opportunity came with a new set of challenges. But I overcame those challenges and very quickly generated some $30 million in additional revenues, which accounted for 40–60 percent of all North American sales.

I attributed this success to having developed strong, trusted relationships with my customers. In an industry that sees a lot of job-hopping and sometimes questionable integrity, I had developed extremely loyal customers because I was diligent, service oriented, trustworthy, and innovative in meeting my customers' needs. I also felt good about the internal relationships I had built.

Throughout my 12-year career at Hypercom, I had worked for six presidents/CEOs—all male. Each treated me with the utmost respect, and all were highly appreciative of my work ethic and lucrative performance. One memorable example came after I had made an unusually large sale. I received an email from the president/CEO who had written: "You are awesome. You are truly appreciated. You have many fans and supporters and I am one of them." Then he nominated me for a national award that resulted in my being named a "Mover and Shaker" by the industry trade publication, *Transaction World Magazine*. The magazine's cover story said in part: "Hypercom asked, 'What do you get when you add one part courageous woman, two parts dynamo, three parts unrelenting determination, four parts exceptional smarts and five parts of a whatever-it-takes attitude?' Their answer, 'You get Lisa Shipley, Senior Vice President and National Sales Director at Hypercom and an industry leader who has changed the POS and ISO marketplace forever.'" The article also stated, "Lisa is beloved and respected by her customers, her sales team and her colleagues. Her colleagues are quick to point out that she never boasts about her accomplishments. They praise her for being the consummate professional, the visionary and the doer." It was a proud moment for me to receive that kind of public praise from my colleagues and to know that I had been nominated for this recognition by the top executive of my company.

There was no question about it. I loved my job!

I was proud to excel for my company and grateful that my successful performance enabled me to provide financial stability for my children. I was pleased that my customers trusted and respected me and that my male colleagues held me in high esteem. I liked being a role model for younger women seeking their own career successes and that I could be an encourager to others who were new to my industry.

I believed so much in what I was doing that the thought never entered my mind that any individual or situation could ever alter my accomplishments, shatter my confidence, or threaten my future success in this industry that I so revered and had been so committed to since its technological birth.

But I was wrong.

- 2 -

CHANGE CREATES CHAOS

It was now 2007, and I had just completed my eleventh year with Hypercom. In February my immediate boss, O. B. Rawls, told me that he would recommend to the CEO that he promote me to senior vice president and managing director of North America. Since he was in charge of global sales and was well aware of the success I had achieved in the United States and Canada, he knew I was ready for this promotion. It was an incredible opportunity. I would be joining the ranks of four men who held the same position in various international markets and it would make me the highest ranking woman in this global, publicly traded company.

Responsibilities for the new role included increasing market share, developing and implementing strategic plans for sales, and managing a national sales team. They were the exact responsibilities of all the other managing directors with the added responsibility for integrated solutions that we provided for large retail stores. This additional aspect of the position entailed a much more complex business environment and one that did not exist in foreign markets. My territory would encompass the company's largest revenue producing territory in the entire world. It was an exciting challenge and one that my previous performance proved I was fully capable of handling.

About the same time as this change was going on, another major change was happening. There were three companies that competed in this industry space—Hypercom, VeriFone, and Ingenico. At this particular time Hypercom was a distant third to the other two, and the board of directors felt that the current president and CEO, as well as his predecessor, had produced very disappointing results. They wanted a different approach. For that reason, they decided to bring on board one of their own—a board member named Philippe Tartavull. Philippe, a native of France who now lived in the United States and held dual citizenship, had demonstrated success running the U.S. operation of Oberthur Card Systems North and Central America, a French credit card company. So in February 2007 the board named Philippe acting president. Organizationally, that placed him directly under the CEO, but the board altered that arrangement by giving Philippe dotted-line authority to report directly to them.

To look at Philippe, you might not immediately get the sense of a strong, powerful executive. He was slender, about 170 pounds, and couldn't have been more than 5 foot 8. His dirty blonde, disheveled hair was cropped close to his head, framing his pale, squared-off, expressionless face. No one seemed to know how he had received the narrow scar that ran from his right temple to the edge of his mouth and exaggerated the severity of his face. He appeared stern and aloof, and when he spoke he never looked you in the eye, and it felt more like he was talking "at" you and deliberately avoiding any real connection. His stiff demeanor and seemingly detached persona sent a chilling warning to anyone who approached him that he was not there as a colleague but more as the one who gets things done. It didn't take long for us to realize that the board had given him complete authority to take full charge.

Besides having Philippe report directly to the board, the CEO had also been stripped of his most important functions—responsibility for global sales, marketing, and product development. The board shifted those responsibilities to Philippe. So although Philippe was technically under the CEO, he was in reality given the authority to manage Hypercom's day-to-day business. It was very clear that Philippe, not the CEO, was now running the show.

Almost immediately Philippe began to implement changes. For example, managing directors were the ones who approved expenses and hired employees without having to seek approval to do so. Philippe put in a new system of expense controls that required his approval for a number of tasks that the managing directors had previously done on their own authority. In essence, he tightened up procedures, thus requiring almost everything to now come through him for his approval.

Throughout this somewhat tumultuous upheaval, my promotion continued to be discussed and in April I officially assumed my new role, fully approved, of course, by Philippe. However, he changed my title from senior vice president to simply managing director. Even though he had approved the position for me, it became evident very early on by his treatment of me that he would have preferred that I had never been promoted. I quickly realized that it was a new day and I would have to prove myself to him. At first this was not a scary prospect to me. I reassured myself that I was well liked by my colleagues and my success with the company was evident. However, this soon gave way to a state of mind at work that bordered on a sense of panic all the time, never knowing when he would direct his next dismissive action at me. In side conversations he was known to refer to me as "junior" managing director. It was very condescending and degrading, but it was only the beginning of many discriminatory tactics that would impact my career and my life.

Although my salary had been decided upon by the time I began my new role, no finalization had been made regarding the remaining elements of my compensation, including commissions, bonus, car allowance, and so on. This impacted me greatly because in the past 11 years those elements in addition to my base salary had accounted for 50 percent of my take-home pay. Thus, without a compensation plan in place my income fell to half of what it should have been.

O.B. tried diligently to finalize this but Philippe refused to deal with it. As a matter of fact, Philippe told O.B. that he had decided he wanted to craft my compensation plan himself; yet as time went on no plan ever developed. I had many conversations with O.B. trying to get my commission structure finalized. He in turn had numerous conversations with Philippe, but to no avail. By the end of April, when I would have normally received my commission, there was no plan in place and so I received nothing. Yet plans for all my male counterparts had been swiftly put in place early in the year. Needless to say, the situation was both frustrating and unfair.

Finally, toward the end of May a plan was provided. My commissions were substantially lower than the company's male managing directors, and worse yet, I still wasn't getting paid my commissions. It wasn't until July that I finally started receiving the commission portion of my pay. During all this time the only one I could get any sympathy or help from was O.B. I constantly complained to him. Not only was I still waiting for compensation I had earned, but I also had been denied car allowances, housing allowances, and stock options that my male peers had all been given. Philippe's excuse was that the disparity was country driven; in other words, for the countries my peers served there were different requirements. I knew this was not the case.

I eventually documented in an email to O.B. that because the payment process had been dragged out for such a long period of time I wanted to personally bring up the issue with Philippe. He was fine with that because he wasn't getting anywhere with him. When I emailed Philippe about the lack of fairness in my compensation his response to me was nothing short of a dismissal. "Lisa, I am starting to be tired of these discussions," he wrote. Again, nothing changed.

By July, none of my commissions had been approved and I again discussed the issue with O.B., who in turn continued to try to get Philippe to do what was right. Philippe's response to O.B. was almost the same. "Don't worry. It's in my court." Then in August, Philippe asked O.B. to leave the company, saying only that he wanted to take the management in a different direction.

Compensation issues, while major, were not the only discriminatory treatment I was receiving. By now it had come to my attention that even my base salary was about $50,000 lower than at least three of the four other managing directors, despite the fact that my territory brought in far greater revenues than any of theirs. I also learned that O.B.'s contract as well as all my male counterparts' contracts had severance agreements worth between three and seven month's pay, while I had been denied one.

Aspects of my being treated differently were no secret. It was well recognized by my peers that Philippe was extremely condescending and disrespectful to me in meetings and even in casual encounters. When we had meetings where all of the managing directors were to make presentations, Philippe would always make me go first and then he would interrupt me, scoff at my suggestions, and purposefully do all he could to diminish my value and embarrass me. While I was giving a presentation at one meeting with all the managing directors from around the world Philippe interrupted me several times. Then he actually left the building in the middle of my presentation. He just walked out. No explanation, no excuse, just walked out. The other managing directors never experienced this treatment. Although Philippe was rude and abrupt to everyone, he was always noticeably more so to me.

Frequently I was excluded from meetings, leaving me feeling humiliated. I was also well aware that out of my presence, my peers would ask O.B. why Philippe treated me the way he did. It was overtly apparent to them that Philippe did not give me the same respect that he gave them. Each week Philippe's dismissive attitude intensified. I lived in fear of what would happen next, believing that Philippe was slowly trying to push me out the door. Over time, despite the fact that I was producing the company's largest revenues, I became emotionally drained and felt like such an outsider. He never granted me a one-on-one meeting the entire time I worked for him; instead, he chose to simply ignore me. To him, I didn't exist. I would go home at night feeling exhausted, and I could feel my confidence eroding as I wondered why I was being treated in this degrading way. After a few months I gave up trying to please Philippe and went into survivor mode, just delivering the numbers in hopes that his attitude toward me would turn around.

||||||||||

The authority I once had to make decisions regarding pricing, deals, expenses, or contracts without explicit approval—Philippe took all that away. Yet when I sought his approval, he simply refused to meet with me—even refused to return my phone calls or emails. When I complained, he dismissed my concerns as "nonsense."

One of the most important ways to promote customer loyalty is for managing directors to take the company president along with them on customer visits. This is particularly important to show appreciation to the company's largest accounts. It's a prestigious gesture that also impacts the ability to increase the sale of Hypercom equipment. In 2007, Philippe visited customers all over the world, working with all of the male managing directors. Despite the fact that I was bringing in contracts valued between $5 million and $25 million with some of the largest companies in the region, no matter how hard I tried to get him to visit any of my customers in the United States, he could not find a single day to visit any of them.

I eventually stopped trying to get him to visit my customers because I knew how much he disliked me and I was worried his disdain for me would become apparent to my customers. I was also concerned his abrupt manner could have been insulting or offensive to my customers.

Despite that, to me there was no rational reason for his refusal to visit my customers other than his out-and-out distaste for me as a female, period. He lived in the United States and travel to any of my customers would have been easy. But he chose to ignore Hypercom's largest customers, which also happened to be mine.

You don't have to be paranoid to feel singled out by this kind of behavior. It was pure dismissive behavior, just like many of the other trivializing things he did to let me know I was not worthy of his time, and just one more way he treated me totally different from any of the other managing directors.

In our industry, like many industries, there are trade shows held every year. Cartes, the one show that potential customers from all over the world attend, was being held in Paris, France, as it was every year. New products are demonstrated at this show; there are educational seminars where new industry developments and trends are discussed; and most important, you have the opportunity to interact with customers and potential customers. Naturally, I expected to attend this show. I inquired numerous times and Philippe's constant response was, "We will decide later." When "later" came, I was not allowed to attend. The reason, supposedly, was "cost." Interestingly, cost had nothing to do with sending my four male peers from around the globe. So, while all of my peers would be afforded the opportunity to mix with potential customers and hear about the latest innovations in the industry, I was left to believe that it was not important for me to do the same. Then when the show was over I found out that Philippe had arranged for a three-hour meeting with all the managing directors on the last day of the show—all the managing directors but me. I could easily have participated in the meeting by phone or Skype, but I was never even given the opportunity. When I later asked Philippe about the meeting, he dismissively responded that I hadn't missed anything.

But, in a later email he freely admitted that one item discussed during this meeting was increasing market share in the United States.

"Missed nothing?" I thought. Here they were discussing increasing the market share of my territory, yet I had absolutely no input. It was yet another example of how Philippe preferred to act as if I didn't exist.

You may be wondering by now why I didn't discuss what was going on with Hypercom's human resources department. Unfortunately, there was no one in the department to discuss my concerns with, as the last manager had left the company in 2006. There were administrative people handling HR issues, but Philippe had reorganized the department so that any decisions regarding these issues had to go directly to him. So, even though I had made my complaints known to superiors, any complaints were simply ignored because they could be. Amazing, but true. Instead of acknowledging any of my concerns, Philippe dismissed them and led superiors to believe that I was just complaining because I didn't like some of the changes he had made.

Clearly, the handwriting was on the wall. I had run out of options. In the months since Philippe had become president the discrimination toward me had progressively intensified, and there were no indications that it would ever improve. In fact, as I would find out later, during this time he had actually interviewed people for my job—a fact he would later vehemently try to deny.

The emotional pressure was immense. Every day I seemed to face another struggle. My drive to succeed and my insecurities about the job kept me fighting for approval. I thought that by bringing in more deals and generating more revenue, maybe I'd get some positive recognition. But the more I succeeded, the more Philippe seemed to dismiss me.

It became clear to me that to stay and fight would be fruitless. At best, I imagined it would only get worse. Soon the stress began affecting my overall health. In fact, one morning I drove to an urgent care center because my heart was racing abnormally fast and I could not seem to get it to stop. It was incredibly frightening. The doctor who examined me found my resting heart rate was 188; the normal resting heart rate for adults ranges from 60 to 100. I was diagnosed with severe stress and put on a heart monitor for a month.

|||||||||||

For years competitors had tried to get me to leave Hypercom and go to work for them; for years I had turned down all offers out of loyalty to the company and a job that I revered. But circumstances had changed and I honestly believed my future was being severely threatened. I had, at the time, received an offer letter from a major competitor and asked myself, Should I accept it or continue to fight the battle?

On December 18, 2007, my decision became absolutely clear. On that day I found out Philippe had been officially named president and CEO of the company. An internal memo went out announcing the appointment and two days later it was announced publicly. Now it was definite— Philippe would be in this position permanently.

That very day I decided to accept the offer I had from Ingenico. I signed the offer letter and on January 3 I resigned from Hypercom in a letter written to the chairman of the board. I wanted the board to know exactly why I was leaving, and I didn't want to allow any opportunity for Philippe to provide his own reasons to board members. I also sent a letter to my staff. I kept it very professional, but I wanted them to hear it from me.

In the past when anyone at Hypercom resigned to go to work for another company they were cut off from everything and escorted out of the building. That did not happen to me. Instead, within a couple of days I received an email requesting me to be in Phoenix—the location of our corporate headquarters—the following Tuesday to meet with Philippe. I agreed to do so and flew to Phoenix.

Philippe stood and greeted me quite cordially, certainly more so than usual. He asked if there was anything that would change my mind. Having little trust that anything I might ask that he would agree to would actually ever happen, I told him no, that too much damage had been done. In his typically cool demeanor, with no direct eye contact, he simply said, "Good," and I felt he was relieved I was definitely leaving.

Philippe then escorted me to the legal department. Here I was given a non-solicit-for-money proposal. If I signed it they would pay me $50,000, but I could not hire any Hypercom employee for the next 12 months. I believed they knew how very loyal my staff was to me and that it would certainly be possible that at some point one of them would want to work for me at Ingenico. I wasn't inclined to sign such an agreement, but I was gracious and said I would review it and left without signing anything. In fact, I never did sign it. At that point my resignation was accepted and I was officially gone from Hypercom—free to begin my new job.

| | | | | | | | | | |

Although I had accepted Ingenico's offer and was now employed by them, I was still legally due commissions for my fourth-quarter sales at Hypercom. Those commissions were to be paid to me in February 2008, along with my final base pay. In my final quarter at Hypercom, I had closed the largest sale in the history of the company—nearly $30 million. In fact, by the end of that year my territory was the largest revenue generator for Hypercom, outproducing all four other regions—regions all led by men.

Based on my fourth-quarter sales, my last paycheck, including base pay and commission, should have totaled about $100,000. To my shock, the check I received was for just $30,000. By my calculations I had been shorted by about $66,000. I was furious. I made several attempts to resolve the shortage issue by communicating with the appropriate people at Hypercom. Despite my attempts to point out that my calculations showed I should have received more, Philippe flatly refused to approve the full amount, insisting that this was all they owed me and nothing would be done to change the decision.

That was the last straw, and I felt that it was just one more part of the blatant discrimination I had been dealing with for the past year. I felt like Philippe was all but daring me to challenge him.

I never had any intention of suing Hypercom when I left; all I wanted was the commission I had rightly earned and to move forward with my life. If I had given any thought to suing the company, I would have done things much differently. As it was, I had turned everything over when I left, all documents, emails, everything that would have provided any evidence of the way I had been treated. Without any of that documentation it would be much more difficult for me to build a case. But now I had been pushed to my limits; I was being cheated financially and that was simply my breaking point. Not paying me what I had rightfully earned felt so unjust that it absolutely pushed me over the edge.

Filing a lawsuit was totally foreign territory for me, something I'd never envisioned doing. I needed advice from someone who knew more about the legal aspects and someone I trusted implicitly. The following month I reached out to a longtime business associate and friend in my hometown of Chicago. For confidentiality purposes, I'm calling him Fred. Fred is an incredibly successful businessman; he is well connected and someone I respect immensely. Fred is also extremely wealthy, and suffice it to say that with all his business transactions through the years he has also had numerous legal dealings.

I discussed my situation with Fred, and he agreed I had been treated unfairly. He also knew that suing a global corporation would be no easy task and that I'd need a very savvy and experienced law firm. He believed that a firm he had personally had many dealings with was the right one. And although I lived in Atlanta and the firm he recommended was in Chicago, he assured me that this should not be a problem.

So, following Fred's sage advice, I contacted the law firm of Neal, Gerber & Eisenberg.

- 3 -

FIGHT BACK—OR RETREAT?

After reviewing all my information, the lawyers at Neal, Gerber & Eisenberg advised me that they thought my case would be a "slam dunk." That led me to believe that it would involve no more than three to six months of legal fees before being settled. So on February 29, 2008, I wrote a letter to the law firm:

"Attached please find an executed Engagement Letter. I look forward to your assistance in determining whether I have merit in asking for damages against Hypercom for gender discrimination. I believe it is important that I share with you some basic background about me and my 12 years of working for Hypercom."

I closed the letter with:

"I really need to understand your thoughts on my ability to fight this issue and what you think the damages may be worth. I left Hypercom with all my stock underwater and I can't fight this too hard on a financial basis if there are not true rewards to be made in the end."

I wanted it to be understood that as much as I wanted to pursue this, I was also not financially equipped to absorb enormous legal costs.

I was told that the entire process would take merely a matter of months. The lawyers seemed to feel I had an airtight case—even that the case would win approximately $900,000. At no time did they sit me down and explain all the possible timelines associated with the process, however. In retrospect, I naively continued to think that at best it would be only a few months before I would be offered some kind of settlement.

I was informed that the place to start was to file a gender discrimination complaint with the Equal Employment Opportunity Commission (EEOC). It was my understanding that at this point companies often decide to settle rather than risk the negative publicity of an actual suit being filed in federal court. So, on June 27, 2008, I filed a gender discrimination complaint with the EEOC.

|| | | | | | | | |

In the heat of emotion, feeling betrayed and wronged, I'm not sure I took the time to explore all the practical and realistic challenges I could potentially face. I was simply focused on achieving some justice for myself. When I signed on with my legal team I had no idea how complicated things might get; how many legal options there would be for Hypercom to drag things out for months—even years; how exceedingly costly it could get; and the additional emotional toll it would eventually exact on me. Only later would I realize what I actually would be up against.

To understand some of the realities I was about to confront, I'd like to share with you some information from the American Bar Foundation—none of which I was aware of at the time I embarked on my own journey. These are some facts about litigation as it relates to employment discrimination lawsuits. These lawsuits, according to the EEOC, include age, disability, equal pay compensation, race/color, sex/gender, retaliation, genetic information, national origin, pregnancy, religion, and sexual harassment.

The foundation's research states that employment discrimination lawsuits are one of the largest categories of civil cases filed in federal court. Although the public mostly hears about class action lawsuits brought against large corporations like Walmart and other well-known entities, these class action suits are extremely rare, accounting for less than 1 percent of the federal caseload. Most employment discrimination lawsuits are actually filed by solo plaintiffs, individuals like me.

In the June 2010 issue of the *Journal of Empirical Legal Studies,* there was an even more disquieting statistic—only 6 percent of those filing employment discrimination lawsuits in federal court ever went to trial. Furthermore, more than 40 percent of those individuals filing lawsuits either had their cases dismissed or lost at summary judgment—when the defendant (the company) asked the court to deny any and all claims filed against them. In other words, the court sided with the employer being sued in nearly three-quarters of the cases filed.

Even when a case does go to trial the chance of winning is a mere one in three, and the cases are often settled for modest settlements. Employers typically do what they can to have these cases dismissed, but when that doesn't work they often offer small or modest settlements, most of which are accepted by the plaintiffs. Of the cases that make it to trial, according to the American Bar Foundation, only one-third of the plaintiffs are successful.

Then there's the added issue of money—what it costs in legal fees to fight the battle. The vast majority of individuals filing these suits can't afford high-powered attorneys. Employers are usually more able to afford lawyers than their employees and can usually afford better, more experienced lawyers. Employees, on the other hand, are generally left with the options of representing themselves, trying to rely on scarce legal aid resources, or finding a lawyer who may be willing to represent them on a contingency basis and take a portion of the settlement or jury award as their payment.

In other words, the odds are generally stacked against the employee from the get-go. It's a steep hill to climb, and unfortunately for legitimate victims of discrimination, it's a peak that can be impossible to cross.

Had I known all these facts up front, would I have started the journey? That's a question I've asked myself over and over. I'm not sure I've settled on a definitive answer.

What I do know is that I believed there would be profound vindication if a jury of my peers would acknowledge that the painful experience I endured was real, inappropriate, and unacceptable. That is what I so desperately needed. That possible outcome is what sustained me as I endured the monumental setbacks that I was about to face.

|||||||||||

Attempts to come to some equitable resolve just didn't happen. It became apparent that Philippe and Hypercom were convinced that they had the upper hand, and for Philippe any hint of settling would merely be an admission of his guilt. He was not about to let that happen. As the CEO, Philippe had been able to convince people that he had never discriminated against me or treated me any differently from anyone else, but rather that I merely didn't like changes he had made so I complained a lot. Now the company was faced with having to defend his explanation. And apparently he was still able to convince company lawyers that he had done nothing discriminatory.

In August I had what can only be described as a "brutal" two-hour call with the EEOC. As we engaged in a discussion about my range of complaints, I felt their interaction with me was indifferent, and at times even downright hostile. Wasn't this the agency that was supposed to be objective—to be neutral rather than combative? Instead, I felt they were doing everything they could to discount my complaints and discourage me so it wouldn't create more workload for them. It was horribly depressing, yet I refused to be dissuaded.

On September 8, 2008, came the next strike. Hypercom wrote to the EEOC filing a response to my EEOC claim stating that it was without merit and therefore requesting that the charge be dismissed in its entirety.

It took two more months of waiting to find out how the EEOC would decide. On November 12, 2008, I received a "Notice of Right to Sue." With that decision the EEOC indicated that they had not sided with either party but felt that there was enough evidence to allow us the right to file a lawsuit in federal court. With that my legal team moved into action and began their preparations.

What I hadn't counted on was that since the trial would be held in Georgia, I needed a Georgia attorney. David Ritter, the lead lawyer with the Chicago firm, was friends with an independent lawyer in Atlanta—Randall (Randy) Grayson. So in January, introductions were made and it was agreed that Randy would be my local Atlanta lawyer. I was then, of course, required to sign a new set of agreements with Randy so he would be paid at the end as well.

Suddenly my legal costs were mounting.

- 4 -

REALITY BITES

I had been paying legal bills for nearly a year now. During all that time I also had my regular family bills as well as the recent expense of Christmas. My legal bills were running between $2,000 and $8,000 a month and there was no settlement in sight. Suddenly it all seemed overwhelming. I knew there was no way I could keep up with the expense. One day I picked up the phone and called my lawyers. I told them I had to stop—despite the fact that I desperately wanted to fight for justice, the money and the stress were simply taking their toll. I had no choice but to call it quits.

I was beginning to grasp the reality of the way this game was played and why so many of these discrimination cases never even make it to trial. The big corporate giants can afford to weather the legal costs, while employees simply can't. It seemed so unfair, yet it was simply the reality. I felt demoralized, disheartened, and defeated by the harsh cold truth. Reality really did bite.

A few days later I got a call from my Chicago lawyers. They wanted to discuss my decision to quit. They told me they had spoken to my Chicago business colleague, Fred. Remember Fred? He was my wealthy business associate and friend in Chicago who had referred me to this law firm in the first place. They said they had talked to Fred and worked out a deal with him that would allow me to stay in the fight and pay him and the lawyers back once the case was settled. They all believed I had a solid case and a good chance of winning if I could just stay the course. I was over the top with excitement because, setting any financial outcome aside, what had always really mattered to me was to prove that this arrogant CEO could not get away with how he had treated me.

So I signed a legal agreement in which Fred would advance my legal fees and expenses. I also signed the agreement to hire Randy as well. I figured that once Randy came on board my expenses with the Chicago firm would diminish. But, as it turned out, that wasn't true. Most of the research needed throughout the case had to be done by the Chicago team. And although Fred agreed to advance money, he did set a cap on the amount he was willing to advance. And for agreeing to provide this advance I had to agree to reimburse him 100 percent of the legal fees and expenses advanced on my behalf plus 25 percent of any remaining settlement proceeds or recovery. If I lost the case entirely, I owed him nothing.

I consider myself to be pretty intelligent and savvy when it comes to the business world. Unfortunately, that wasn't the case with the legal world. In hindsight, having no experience with lawsuits, the truth is that I really never fully understood the terms of either agreement or just how much of any gross settlement I might get would go to the lawyers and Fred. Plus, I was so emotionally hurt by all I had gone through and wanted to believe that if the lawyers believed I had a good chance, I had to believe it too. In retrospect, I guess I was so blinded by wanting to right the wrong that I didn't take time to fully understand all the financial consequences. The only thing I knew for sure at this point was that this was going to be a journey of twists and turns with an unpredictable timeline and erratic actions from Hypercom.

When you are so committed to fight for what you believe is right you just can't stop, you can't abandon the fight. That's why I probably would have signed anything if I thought I could possibly end up with some element of justice.

|||||||||||

My lawsuit against Hypercom alleged that the company had violated Title VII of the Civil Rights Act by discriminating against me on the basis of gender and had violated the Georgia Wage Payment laws, the Equal Pay Act, and Georgia law by paying me lower compensation based on gender. It sought compensatory damages for emotional distress, damage to reputation, embarrassment, lost wages, back pay, accrued interest, punitive damages, attorney's fees and expenses, and interest. Once filed, it didn't take long for me to realize that in the legal system there are many legal ways to cause delays—all of which not only drag out the process but rack up legal costs as well.

One month later—February 2009—Hypercom filed a motion to dismiss my lawsuit, claiming that the company had never done business in Georgia and thus my suit had been filed in an improper venue. They also claimed that none of the alleged discriminatory activities detailed in my complaint were committed in Georgia, but rather that my employment records were maintained and administered in Arizona. Finally the motion stated that Hypercom closed its Georgia office in July 2008 and no longer operated an office in the state; therefore, the case should be dismissed or moved to Arizona.

The fact was that while the corporation's headquarters may have been located in Arizona, Hypercom had paid for an Atlanta office for me and others for more than ten years. But somehow they left that piece of information out of their motion. According to my lawyers, the real reason Hypercom wanted the case moved to Arizona was because the laws were more favorable to employers in that state. Regardless, I was in Georgia and we wanted the case to be fought in Georgia. So in March, my lawyers filed a response stating that in fact throughout my career I had worked out of a fully equipped Atlanta office provided by Hypercom, and we provided the specific address. We then cited court cases supporting our contention that the suit not be moved to Arizona, quoting such court decisions as "The plaintiff's choice of forum should not be disturbed unless it is clearly outweighed by other considerations."

At the end of May the court issued a report and recommendation denying Hypercom's motion to change the venue and conveyed that if there were any further objections they would have to be filed within a ten-day period. No objections were filed within the required period of time, so in June, four months after Hypercom's request for dismissal or move of venue, the federal court denied Hypercom's motion, allowing the case to go forward in the Atlanta court as originally filed. Nearly six months had now passed and we were nowhere near finding out if the case would ever get to trial. My legal bills were rapidly rising, running approximately $8,000 a month. The stress was enormous and we weren't even at trial. So much for settling within a few months.

At the end of June 2009, Hypercom accepted that the Atlanta venue was proper but now denied all other allegations in my suit. Once again the company asked that the court dismiss the suit in its entirety. So began a new set of back-and-forth filings that caused additional delays. It would be February 2010, more than a year after I filed my lawsuit, before the court denied this request also.

Late in the fall of 2010, in the middle of all the other back-and-forth legal filings, Hypercom blindsided me, and my legal team, by filing their own lawsuits. Not only did they sue me personally, they also sued two former Hypercom employees who had been hired by Ingenico 20 months after I had joined Ingenico.

We were all stunned; it seemed unprecedented. Hypercom was now coming after me personally as well as the company I had gone to work for. They were also coming after two innocent men who had left Hypercom and joined me at Ingenico. To me this was pure retaliation for the lawsuit I had filed against them, and I had to ask myself, How ugly is this going to get?

Unfortunately, it looked like things were going to get very ugly. It was also embarrassing and nerve-racking. Here I was in a new job at a new company—still feeling completely humiliated by Hypercom. Plus, I also was enduring the stressful burden of knowing that the two men for whom I had the utmost respect and admiration were going through this turmoil with me. Many other employees before them had left Hypercom and gone to work for competitors without a problem. Since I hadn't had a noncompete agreement myself, I assumed that neither of them did either. In retrospect I should have asked. But I didn't. It was an oversight I was now regretting.

I never could have predicted just how ugly a fight it would turn out to be. After all, who could have ever guessed that in the middle of it all I would be personally accused of doing unconscionable things and my company and two innocent colleagues would be accused of unlawful actions as well.

Certainly this unthinkable action by Hypercom was pure retaliation, yet it was an action that had yet to be dealt with.

- 5 -

ALL BETS ARE OFF

Ingenico had extended job offers to Bernie Frey and Greg Boardman, both of whom had worked for me previously. They had excelled in their positions at Hypercom, and we had a great rapport. I began serious discussions with the two men earlier in the year about joining me at Ingenico. I assumed neither had ever signed a noncompete agreement because these were so rare in our industry. Rather, it was extremely common that people would move from one company to another and this should be no exception.

Greg had been on the product side of Hypercom. He's brilliant with process and workflow, and a diehard Alabama fan. He's a short, stocky guy with a giant elephant tattooed on his entire upper arm, and he's got a heart of gold.

Bernie is slim built and a rather eccentric guy who is absolutely solid—someone you can totally count on. He had been on the sales side.

When it was decided that Ingenico would make an offer to these two it was determined that Greg would report to my boss, Chris Justice, and would manage the product/software side of the business. Bernie would report to me and run the sales operation for the banking clients. The offers went out from Ingenico's human resources department in August 2009, and Bernie and Greg began to make their plans to leave Hypercom.

Both men were very aware that when I left Hypercom, I had never been paid the full commissions I had earned. They knew about the lawsuit and that not being paid was the impetus for me filing it. As a result, Bernie was adamant about waiting until his paycheck that closed out the previous Hypercom quarter was actually paid. Greg decided to wait as well and resign at the same time. Bernie received his commission on Friday, August 7, 2009, and both men gave notice to Hypercom the following Monday, August 10.

That's what caused all hell to break loose for them.

|||||||||||

Nothing could have been more unpredictable or felt more like retaliation than when "out of the blue" in September lawsuits started arriving from Hypercom.

First suits were filed against Bernie and Greg, asking for injunctions to stop them from going to work at Ingenico. The suit against Greg, filed on August 14, 2009, in Superior Court of Arizona, Maricopa County, alleged that prior to his resignation from Hypercom, he and Ingenico—a competitor—conspired to solicit Hypercom employees to join Ingenico and that he misappropriated, and continued to misappropriate, trade secrets and other confidential information belonging to Hypercom. They claimed he did this in knowing violation of a written agreement between him and Hypercom. As a result, Hypercom alleged that the company suffered significant and irreparable harm and damages and would continue to do so unless granted temporary, preliminary, and permanent injunctive relief against any ongoing violations. They further argued that Greg had signed a Confidentiality, Non-Solicitation, and Non-Compete Agreement with Hypercom in 2008, and claimed that

I, Lisa Shipley, knew of this agreement. The fact is, I didn't know. Only later did I find out that he had actually signed one and that it had been so long since he had signed it that he had actually forgotten about it. I accepted that and let it go.

What was particularly defamatory to Greg was that Hypercom also claimed that following a "limited forensic review" of Greg's electronic and hard-copy records, they believed and alleged that he engaged in an intentional scheme to misappropriate trade secrets and other highly confidential and/or proprietary information from Hypercom—presumably for his own benefit and that of his new employer.

Shortly thereafter, on August 17, 2009, Hypercom filed a suit in the Court of Common Pleas of Allegheny County, Pennsylvania, against Bernie, alleging that he had violated an Employee Confidentiality and Non-Disclosure Agreement he had signed on the day he was hired and that he, I, and others at Ingenico conspired to misappropriate trade secrets and other highly confidential and/or proprietary information both before and after his resignation. They also accused him of renegotiating his compensation plan when he knew he would be leaving Hypercom, enabling him to be compensated with an additional payment on the Friday before he "abruptly" resigned. They further alleged that there was a substantial threat that Bernie had already disclosed, or would disclose, confidential customer information, trade secrets, and other confidential and proprietary information.

Ingenico was named as a defendant in both suits, thereby causing the company to legally defend its role in all of this as well.

||||||||||

Everyone was shocked that Hypercom had come after Bernie and Greg. But the greater shock for me came a few weeks later. I was in Denver on a business trip when my son told me that a "very scary man in a black pickup truck" was looking for me and had been camped in front of our house and wouldn't leave. Needless to say, having no idea why this man would be looking for me, I was worried. Two days later when I got home, he was still there. But when he saw me pull into my driveway, he got out, approached me, and handed me some papers.

When I finally read the document, I was in absolute shock. Apparently Hypercom was now suing me—personally. To fully understand some of the legalistic terminology, I had to ask my lawyers to explain it in laymen's terms.

Conspiracy? Theft?

How outrageous! How malicious!

Again I felt humiliated—like a common criminal—and that I'd done something so terrible that the law was coming after me. Among other allegations, they charged that I had acted in concert with Bernie and Greg and others at Ingenico to conspire to misappropriate Hypercom's trade secrets and other confidential and proprietary information for personal benefit and that of Ingenico. They further alleged that I intentionally and/ or purposefully interfered with Hypercom's valid business relationships with fraud, malice, and/or oppression, which would result in economic injury to Hypercom—and that I had caused Bernie and Greg to breach their respective fiduciary duties with Hypercom.

In other words—I was a thief and I had knowingly conspired with Bernie and Greg to ruin Hypercom. It was crazy, but it was just one more personally degrading and demeaning action to add to the disrespect I had experienced while working for Philippe.

There was one other interesting aspect of Hypercom's suit against me. Unlike the suits the company had filed against Bernie and Greg, where they had named Ingenico as a defendant, they did not name Ingenico in the suit against me. Obviously, they didn't want Ingenico named as a defendant because that would enable Ingenico to be involved in my case and potentially provide support for me.

I was convinced this was retaliatory and just another one of Philippe's personal vendettas. I was terrified thinking of the personal consequences.

With everything becoming public record, this could ruin my reputation in the industry in which I had spent my entire professional career. Also, with Hypercom being a publicly traded company that filed quarterly reports with the Securities and Exchange Commission, they were required to report detailed information about the lawsuit—details that would become public record as well.

Because of the stigma about gender discrimination cases, particularly among the men—and my industry was already packed with "good ole boys"—in some respects I already felt like a bit of an outcast. I feared people's impressions of me would change. I hated that. I desperately needed—and wanted—to fit in. And whether these feelings were imaginary or real, they began to erode my confidence even more.

How hateful and vindictive could Philippe and Hypercom actually be? How could I have such an evil enemy? The depth to which I now believed Philippe was willing to go to get back at me was utterly inconceivable. Quite frankly, it scared me to death.

As if things weren't stressful enough with the uncertainties of my own lawsuit, I was now being forced to defend my personal integrity. Added to that was the anguish of seeing two people I respected—and a company that had entrusted their faith in me—suffering because of me. It was an absolute nightmare. The emotional impact of it all was excruciating. But there was one thing my lawyers said I could do—I could amend my lawsuit to indicate that Hypercom's suit against me personally was a retaliation suit that constitutes unlawful retaliation in violation of Title VII of the Civil Rights Act. Thus, on September 9, 2010, we filed a motion asking the court's permission to file an amended complaint to our suit, claiming that Hypercom had filed a retaliatory and baseless lawsuit against me. On October 20 the magistrate judge granted the motion, and this was officially added to my original suit.

|||||||||||

Everyone at Ingenico was supportive, especially my boss, Chris Justice, the president of Ingenico. What a perfect last name. Not only was this man the epitome of a sophisticated, well-spoken corporate president, he had the integrity and dedication of Superman.

Ingenico filed a request to the judge to allow them to be a party to my suit. The good news was that the court granted the request. The bad news was that as a result there were things Ingenico simply had to do that made life more difficult for me. Despite the company's support of me, until my case was decided, they had to put some restrictions on how freely I could operate. They required that I could no longer have any communication with Bernie or Greg. This was a killer for me emotionally; I couldn't even check on them or let them know how badly I felt.

|||||||||||

Because of the court injunction, all plans for Bernie and Greg to go to work for Ingenico were put on hold, and therefore they each had to hire and pay for their own lawyers. Also, all my work-related belongings were sequestered. My laptop was taken so Ingenico's people could look for documents that Hypercom had subpoenaed, including all communications between me and just about everyone I'd ever communicated with. Not only did they want my Ingenico emails, they wanted everything from my personal emails as well.

Like a lot of people, I had deleted very little from either my professional or personal accounts. I had years of emails on Google Cloud and my hard drive was pretty full. I started reading all the emails that Hypercom had subpoenaed. I was making myself crazy wondering how they might be twisted and turned against me. Even emails that had nothing to do with Hypercom might be taken out of context and used against me. Sorting through all of this consumed me; I could think of nothing else as I fretted over all the possibilities. My family and work fell to the wayside, and I was totally engulfed in trying to see if, in fact, there was any kind of "smoking gun." In my heart I knew I had done nothing wrong, but in my head I could not shake the possibility that some little thing might end up being damaging. I was obsessed, exhausted, and emotionally drained.

As time went on the emotional pain of not being able to talk to Bernie and Greg intensified. With all my phone records and emails having been subpoenaed, I knew that future emails and phone records would likely be subpoenaed as well. Thus, I couldn't even make a personal phone call to either of them. I was particularly concerned about Bernie. He's extremely sensitive and above all a man of great integrity; it's what I love most about him. He holds confidences to a fault and now he was being dragged through the mud, accused of things that challenged his integrity. I knew how unbearably painful that was for him and I wanted desperately to reach out and provide some comfort and reassurance to him. But I couldn't.

Finally, I confess, the anguish of thinking about what both colleagues were going through became unbearable. One of my brothers was living in Canada at the time and his last name was different from mine. I knew a call from him would be safe and not raise a red flag, so I asked him to call both Bernie and Greg and tell them that I knew everything was going to be okay, that I was so sorry they were being dragged into this, and that I cared about and respected them. I wanted to encourage them to hang in there and to let them know that Ingenico was on their side and would do everything they could to fight this to the end.

After delivering the messages my brother called to tell me Bernie and Greg were very happy that he had called. It felt so clandestine. But it was also a huge relief to know that they knew I was thinking of them and that I cared.

| | | | | | | | | |

Those of us from Ingenico were advised that Greg's case would be the first one up. It would be held in Phoenix where Greg lived and where

Hypercom's corporate offices were located. I was going to be allowed to testify. We had only a week or two to prepare before flying to Phoenix. We knew Greg's case would be tricky because we had found out that, unbeknownst to any of us, when Greg left Hypercom he had actually taken some documents he didn't believe were confidential in nature. Hypercom disagreed.

I testified in a hearing held on September 2 regarding a preliminary injunction to enforce Greg's non-compete agreement with Hypercom. At issue was the enforceability of the Confidentiality, Non-Solicitation, and Non-Compete Agreement.

On September 8, the court issued its ruling, vacating the temporary injunction and denying Hypercom's application, finding that "restriction for all of North America is oppressive, unreasonable, and against Arizona public policy." The court further found that Greg had learned "some" confidential information but that he had testified that he had no desire to harm Hypercom and disclose the information. An interesting aside was the fact that Greg's wife worked for Hypercom and would continue to work there.

The court agreed with Greg's position and declared "the unsubstantiated threat of disclosure is not enough for a plaintiff to meet its burden of proof to warrant injunctive relief at this time," and ruled in favor of Greg, dropping all charges against him.

In the end, Ingenico agreed to wait out the non-compete agreement that we hadn't known existed. They rehired Greg as soon as it expired. Subsequently, the suit against Bernie was dropped, but what they put him through was criminal in my opinion. He was so ready for his day in court. He wanted his name cleared, and he wanted his chance to look Philippe in the eye and testify how Philippe had lied and treated him. When they dropped his case he was relieved on the one hand, but he was upset that he never got his day in court.

With those two cases dismissed, the case against Ingenico as a defendant was also dismissed. As for me, after Hypercom's losing efforts with these two cases, along with the fact that after analyzing laptops, phone records, and everything else they could get their hands on, the company found absolutely nothing to support their accusations and dropped my suit as well. But they did it "without prejudice," which means that they could choose to refile the case at any time in the future. Thus, while the suit was dropped, I felt that the potential threat continued to loom.

By early November, Hypercom had filed its answer to my amended complaint, denying that their suit against me had been a retaliation suit. I would still have to wait to see how the court would decide. Was I right, or did the court think Hypercom was right?

At this juncture, there was no turning back. But, again, I had to ask myself just how long this would drag on. What unexpected actions were still to come? And, how much was this really going to cost me? The uncertainty of it all became undeniably clear. All I could hope for was that my financial backer wasn't watching to see how near we were getting to the cap he had set.

- 6 -

FIGHTING DIRTY

At last I could now get back to some normalcy at my job. I didn't feel completely at ease, knowing that at any time in the future Hypercom could refile their suit against me. But for right now I figured they had probably decided to focus on the bigger suit at hand. I was right. In November they filed their answer to my amended allegation of their unlawful retaliation. Of course, they denied all the allegations.

Three weeks later Hypercom filed another motion regarding the retaliation claim, arguing that I had failed to exhaust the administrative process required by not first filing the retaliation complaint with the EEOC. Therefore, they asked that my retaliation claim be dismissed. My attorneys filed a motion opposing Hypercom's request, alleging that they had misconstrued the facts. Fourteen days later, on March 15, the court denied Hypercom's motion, agreeing that I should not have had to first go to the EEOC. Thus, the court agreed with me and the retaliation amendment remained a part of my lawsuit.

Given all the tactics Hypercom had used to try to delay things, it was anyone's guess what they might do next. But with things now appearing to move forward, it was time for depositions. Depositions are important to the lawyers on both sides. The content provides information directly related to the lawsuit from several individuals. Some depositions are longer than others, and what is said in the deposition must be concurrent with what the person later says as a witness. During the trial if anyone contradicts something he or she said in the deposition on the witness stand, the deposition will be called into play. In some instances, questions asked in the deposition may not be asked at trial. It just depends on how the lawyers view the respective responses.

When Hypercom's lawyer asked O.B. to describe Philippe, O.B. mentioned that he didn't think Philippe liked having a woman report to him.

"It was not his style," O.B. said. *"He was very French in his attitude."*

When asked what he meant by that O.B. replied, *"Disrespectful towards business associates, very self-centered, very focused on his own needs and not caring about the business needs of the people there."*

A bit later in the deposition the lawyer asked O.B. if he had ever told Philippe that I had told him I felt I was being treated differently as a woman. He responded, *"I told Philippe at one point but he said it was nonsense. That was his answer."*

"Did he say anything else?" the lawyer probed. *"Do you know how long that conversation lasted?"*

I love O.B.'s response.

"Doesn't take long to say 'nonsense,' does it?"

That one, brief statement pretty much said it all when it came to how little Philippe cared about dealing with me or any of my concerns.

||||||||||

Hypercom continued to cause unnecessary delays, even making it difficult to move forward with some of the depositions. First were motions for extension of time—an acceptable legal request, yet also a legitimate way to stall things. But even more frustrating was the fact that Hypercom failed to provide documents requested by my lawyers—documents that contained pertinent information needed in order to responsibly move forward with our depositions.

Because of all these delays a five-page letter was sent to the Hypercom lawyers from my lawyers expressing the frustration. In part, here is what was written, and it demonstrates just how uncooperative Hypercom was:

"Hypercom's failure to fully respond is frustrating, to say the least, particularly in light of the fact that you have agreed to produce certain categories of responsive documents (such as internal communications) but have not delivered.

"We have repeatedly asked for a 'back log report' as of the end of the fourth quarter in 2007/beginning of first quarter in 2008.

"Hypercom continues to deny that it has or can create such a report. However, as emailed to you on March 16, Clint Jones [Hypercom's chief of staff] *testified during his deposition about the existence of a backlog report. Mr. Tartavull also testified about such a report. Mr. Jones specifically testified that copies of these reports are provided to the Board of Directors after the close of each quarter. He further testified that the accounting department would have documents about inventory. Equally important, both Mr. Tartavull and Mr. Jones adamantly testified that the company has controls that prevent Hypercom from manipulating its earnings by delaying the shipment of products in inventory and both identified accounting records that they believed could be used to evidence their assertions.*

"It is frustrating to be repeatedly told by you that Hypercom does not have such documents only to have two of Hypercom's high-ranking officers testify at length about them."

The letter went on to state Hypercom's additional failures to produce other requested documents, noting that for many of the requested documents this was the third set of requests. The letter ended by proposing that both parties agree to a "brief extension of discovery," and that in the absence of that agreement, *"We must request a conference with the magistrate regarding the numerous outstanding discovery issues and seek guidance from the Court."*

In essence, this was one more example of Hypercom's intentional, yet legal way to stall the proceedings.

|||||||||||

I had learned that earlier when I was trying to get Philippe to finalize my compensation and address my various concerns he had actually been trying to replace me, a situation that no one seemed to want to confirm. But, at the end of March a declaration was received from a woman. Because I prefer to respectfully protect her identity I will call her Barbara. What was important about this was that the declaration supported my contention that Philippe had been interviewing someone for my position during the period of time that he was totally ignoring my concerns. Here are some of the pertinent statements made by Barbara in her declaration:

"I was first contacted by Mr. Tartavull (Philippe) in early December 2007. Mr. Tartavull stated that, although we had never met, he had heard good things about me from a member of Hypercom's Board and from my reputation in the industry. At that time, he asked me if I would be interested in the position in charge of all of Hypercom's sales in the North American territory. I knew this position was then held by Lisa Shipley ('Ms. Shipley').

"I asked Mr. Tartavull about Ms. Shipley's employment status. Based on his response, I understood that Ms. Shipley was unhappy and would not be at Hypercom for much longer.

"I expressed interest in Ms. Shipley's position, and Mr. Tartavull called me back in December 2007, and offered me the position then held by Ms. Shipley. The offer consisted of base salary, stock options and other compensation incentives."

Barbara noted that she turned down the offer, citing that it was monetarily insufficient to entice her to leave her current position. When Philippe advised her that the board of directors had authorized a larger monetary package, she again rejected the offer. But, she said Philippe didn't let it end there.

"Mr. Tartavull and I spoke by telephone a number of times in December 2007 and continuing through early January 2008 about the position. Mr. Tartavull was persistent and seemed hopeful that I would accept his offer."

But once again she declined the offer and remained in her current position until she retired.

This declaration absolutely confirmed that instead of trying to resolve my concerns, Philippe was instead trying to replace me. Here I was, continuing to bring in business and succeeding at record pace, and all the while, instead of valuing my efforts, he was scheming behind my back to replace me. And, he apparently thought he was protecting himself by replacing me with another woman so it would never look like he had anything against me based on my gender. It was typical of how scheming he could be.

By now it was July 2010. Here came the next stall. Hypercom filed a motion for summary judgment asking that my entire case be thrown out. They claimed that I had no evidence to establish a hostile work environment because I could show no cause to establish that the circumstances caused me to resign; therefore, as a matter of law, I could not establish a retaliation claim. They further claimed that I could not, as a matter of law, establish a case of discrimination under the Equal Pay Act. In summary, they claimed, my complaints were merely about management style, hurt feelings, and unhappiness because of changes in corporate policy.

I failed "miserably," they said, to develop evidence that would prove a hostile work environment. Therefore, they contended, the court should enter a judgment for Hypercom on all counts. In other words, my entire case had no validity, so throw it out.

When I found this out I couldn't understand why something that seemed so black and white to me and my lawyers could be so invisible—

even inconceivable—to Hypercom. As time passed and more unexpected delays materialized I again began questioning myself. Was I so wrong? Did I just *think* Philippe had treated me worse than he had? Was this kind of treatment just acceptable in the corporate world? Had I taken this all too personally?

The answer to all questions was no. I reeled in my doubts and remembered the facts. The facts absolutely confirmed that yes, without a doubt, Philippe had created a hostile work environment for me, and no, he did not treat me fairly. The facts were all there and certainly would at some point prevail; surely these tactical delays would soon come to an end and I would get my day in court.

Throughout the delays I tried to preserve as much normality to life as I could, striving to maintain a strong level of performance at work and struggling to keep some level of normalcy intact for my family. But it was difficult. The case took so much of my time and energy that often it was impossible to concentrate on anything. Needless to say, I was distracted.

When I would see an email come through from my lawyers, my heart would just sink, not knowing what problem or concern might be revealed. When the message was problematic or about something negative, I couldn't get it out of my mind and obsessed about it for the rest of the day. Rarely did I get good news from my lawyers. Generally it was about more delays or more accusations. It was exhausting. And there seemed to be no end in sight.

When I would go home at night I would find myself totally preoccupied by the day's events. I was often short with my kids. And all I could talk about was the agony I was going through. I knew it had to make everyone around me crazy. I'd try to take my mind away from it by hosting a dinner party or engaging in some other activity. But even then I'd find myself talking too much about the lawsuit. Later I'd think about what friends or colleagues really thought, and I was convinced that while the women probably believed me, many of the men probably didn't. Because of the negative stigma attached to "discrimination" cases I was convinced that most men simply would never believe the validity of my case. Irrational or not, it was depressing. It shook my confidence even more, thrusting me into a whirlwind cycle of doubt, second-guessing myself, and continually questioning, Am I really doing the right thing?

Just when I was starting to unravel, I'd have a flash of reality, tell myself that yes, this was the right thing to do, and stoically trudge through another day.

The one question that never seemed to go away, however, was, What other possible delay tactics would Hypercom use to drag this out? Surely these delays would have to come to an end and this case would soon go to trial, wouldn't it?

- 7 -

JUST WHEN I THOUGHT THINGS COULD NOT GET WORSE

A few changes transpired during the time the lawsuit was in process. For one thing, I left Ingenico in April 2011 after the president of First Data Corporation reached out to me and offered me a job. First Data had been Hypercom's largest client and was also a client of Ingenico. After all I had been through I thought it might be a good idea to work on the other side of the business—the client side. My boss at Ingenico was fully supportive and wished me well.

Also in the fall of 2010, in the midst of all this turmoil, VeriFone, a San Jose–based rival of Hypercom, attempted a hostile takeover of Hypercom. This action was something my lawyers and I had to watch very carefully because of its potential impact on my case going forward.

The takeover effort received major regulatory scrutiny. If these two companies became one, it would account for more than half of the U.S. market selling electronic payment terminals. The takeover didn't happen immediately, but in August 2011 VeriFone did acquire Hypercom after both companies reached a settlement with the U.S. Department of Justice whereby Hypercom divested its U.S. payment systems business.

At first my lawyers and I thought this acquisition was great news, that it should be good for our case. We thought that VeriFone would make Hypercom settle their outstanding lawsuits, not wanting to inherit Hypercom's dirty laundry. But that was not the case. We were aware that Hypercom had insurance money put aside for pending lawsuits, so our guess was that Hypercom convinced VeriFone that the insurance would cover any potential lawsuit costs. Once VeriFone inherited my lawsuit, things became even more complicated. I was now working for First Data and we were VeriFone's largest customer. Talk about awkward.

In some ways, I thought this might be a blessing. First Data's president knew all about my case and was fully supportive of me. So he called VeriFone's CEO personally and suggested to him that they drop the case. "You have no dog in this hunt," he told him. "And now you are picking on one of my own." He reached out to the VeriFone CEO on multiple occasions, even letting him know that if the case went to trial, he would be testifying on my behalf. Amazingly, his requests landed on deaf ears. No offers to settle ever came from VeriFone, even though an earlier court decision made it look like there was a strong chance this suit would go to trial.

So much time had passed and legal costs continued to mount. My fear of the ongoing bills was that if I lost at trial and Fred ended up paying more than he had agreed to pay he could come after me for the difference. Knowing Fred, he probably would, and that was a risk that continually lingered in the back of my mind.

In February, prior to the VeriFone acquisition, word had come from the court on Hypercom's motion for Summary Judgment back in July 2010, where they had requested that my whole suit be thrown out. The federal judge recommended granting Hypercom's motion to exclude from the lawsuit the sexual harassment hostile work environment claim, the constructive discharge claim, and the Georgia wage payment statute claim. But he denied Hypercom's motion to discharge my claims for disparate treatment, retaliation, and Equal Pay Act and Georgia Sex Discrimination in Employment Act claims, thus ruling in my favor for these issues.

In March the court adopted the magistrate judge's recommendations. In other words, the critical portions of my case would stand.

But like a dog with a bone, Hypercom refused to let go. The company filed a motion claiming that when the court had ruled in my favor on keeping the retaliation portion of the suit in my case, they hadn't protested the ruling, and they now wanted to do so.

Fortunately, that tactic failed. The court denied that motion too and instead ordered that both parties move forward toward setting a trial date and that we each had 30 days to submit joint pretrial orders. In other words, no more delays from Hypercom. They now had to proceed with the necessary documentation to go to trial. Two years, two months, and eight days had now passed since I had filed my original lawsuit.

A pretrial conference was held on May 19 where both parties agreed to proceed to trial and a tentative date of October 17 was set. Only six days later the trial date was reset for December 5, 2011.

At the end of June, realizing that the suit was actually going to trial, Hypercom made me an offer in the amount of $125,000. After all this time and all they had put me through, I found the offer to be an absolute insult—a slap in the face. As you might expect, we did not respond. Because the offer was not accepted within 14 days it expired. We would now proceed to trial. My absolute focus from here on out would be to prepare for the trial.

I could hardly believe it. At last I would have my day in court!

|||||||||

My lawyers told me that preparing for trial was going to be a full-time job between now and the start of the court proceedings. I went to my boss and told him that for all intents and purposes I would be out of pocket for at least 90 days. Fortunately (and a little unbelievably), he understood and assured me of his full support. I finally felt like I was turning a corner.

At this point the lawyers thought if there was any possibility that VeriFone might settle instead of incurring the cost of actually going to trial that would be a viable option to consider. But since the lawyers couldn't legally contact VeriFone's lawyers because we were in the middle of this lawsuit, they suggested that I reach out to the head of legal at VeriFone as a last-ditch effort to see if they would settle. Even though Hypercom had made a pitiful offer earlier, we were now dealing with VeriFone. They hadn't caused the suit so perhaps they would be relieved to settle. We thought that if I made a personal effort to approach a settlement, it might be something they were now ready to do. So I put a call into VeriFone's head of legal. He wasn't available so I left a message and waited for a call back.

The day he returned the call, I happened to be walking down the street in midtown Manhattan. I looked for a somewhat quiet place to take the call and ducked into the entrance of a closed shop. I asked him—really begged him—to settle. I offered him a settlement amount that I had previously discussed with my lawyers. But he wasn't interested—not at all. He told me that on the advice of company lawyers they still believed my case had no merit, and they would proceed to trial.

I could hardly believe his response. I was livid. Their attitude was no different from that of Hypercom. Despite all the court's rulings and ordering the case to trial, and despite the fact that this was not even their case to begin with, they still chose to believe that my case had no merit! It seemed implausible.

I was so angry I couldn't contain myself. Before hanging up I told him that this would be a battle on the witness stand between Philippe and me and I WOULD shine! "I'll tell my story and I'm confident that the jury will believe me, not him," I avowed. "That Georgia jury will loathe his arrogance and snobbish accent, and I will bring him down!"

As I hung up I felt incensed, yet it motivated me like never before to continue the fight. Their unwillingness to even consider a settlement and their overconfidence were incomprehensible—it provoked me and heightened my energy. I now needed to prepare for all-out war. For the first time in a long time I was pumped.

|||||||||||

My lawyer and I met regularly by phone for the first month or so. There were many long, extended conversations. Later we decided we needed a full week together, locked in a room, to intensely prepare. Prepping for a trial is a lot like writing a book: you have to determine a strategy for how you're going to lay out the story to the jury, identify key points you want to be sure to make, and decide how to continuously illustrate those critical points. Hours were spent anticipating what VeriFone's lawyers might say or do and strategizing how we would respond. We would go witness by witness and call them in to prep them for the questions they would be asked by us. We would also anticipate questions that they might be asked by the defending lawyers and prep them for those. They had to be comfortable with whatever they might be asked.

Some witnesses met with us in our "war room," while we worked with others over the phone. We had sticky notes and sheets of paper with notations plastered all over the conference room. It looked like a military plan. And in a way it was. It was our plan to fight my war.

In November, one month before the trial date, as I was continuing to prepare myself my lawyers had to fight new legal issues that VeriFone's lawyers brought before the court. VeriFone's lawyers had filed a motion to exclude certain evidence of my "alleged" compensatory damages claim. They were also asking the court to exclude certain evidence of my "alleged" damages relating to my claim of retaliation as well as to evidence and references related to my dismissed Title VII claims. Each of these motions had to be answered by my lawyers as well as the defendant's objection to exhibits that my attorneys had notified the court they would be using in the trial.

Now that we were nearing the actual trial date, VeriFone's lawyers seemed to be trying to eliminate the presentation of anything that might potentially be seen by the jury as negative for them. In the end, the court granted some motions but others were denied.

We were now down to the wire and preparation intensified.

My lawyers absolutely drilled me. They knew I would be on the stand for a full day or two and that everything I said and how I said it would be critical. They drilled me not only with questions they planned to ask but also with those they anticipated would be asked by the defending lawyers. It was grueling. But it was necessary. Even when I was on my own I would ask myself the questions and answer out loud so I would become acutely aware of what and how I answered. I was finally beginning to feel more comfortable with all I'd be asked. All the questions, that is, except for the final questions from my own lawyers.

Randy, my Atlanta lawyer who would be the one questioning me, said he would ask two last questions when I was on the stand but did not want to hear my responses until the day I was testifying. I was not to give too much thought to my answers, he said, because they needed to be spontaneous and "come from your heart." The two questions were: When you were going through all the discrimination while at Hypercom, how did it affect you then and now? How did the whole process of going through this lawsuit affect you?

As I continued to prepare for trial and speak my answers to potential questions out loud, I would simply choke up when I would get to those last two questions. I realized even if I wanted to rehearse them, I couldn't. My heart would become heavy, tears would well up in my eyes, and I could not wrap my mind around how I would answer those two questions. I simply had to trust Randy and know that when the time came I would find the right words. I would just speak from the heart.

I was now ready. At long last, it was showtime. My day in court had arrived.

- 8 -

MY DECEMBER D-DAY

It was a cloudy day in Atlanta, Georgia, on Monday, December 5, 2011. The temperature was predicted to reach the upper 60s by afternoon— unusual for a normally colder, chilly day at this time of year. Perhaps that was a good omen. Finally, after three and a half tumultuous years of delays since filing my gender discrimination case with the EEOC we were actually going to trial. It had been 1,256 days to the day to be exact—days in which I had felt demeaned, humiliated, unduly challenged, wrongfully accused, severely stressed, and downright lied to. I was finally getting my day in court. This was my D-day. My trial was actually going to begin.

As I approached the Richard B. Russell Federal Court building in downtown Atlanta, I was full of nervous energy and adrenaline. Being a federal court building the lines were long with everyone waiting to go through security. Ahead of me I could see VeriFone's (Hypercom's) team of lawyers.

I was grateful that finally a jury of my peers would hear for themselves the actual facts of why I believed I had been so unfairly treated. I was also apprehensive. There was so much unknown about how the jury would respond to the testimony and how they would actually decide after all was said and done. Still, I was excited and cautiously optimistic and hopeful.

After clearing security I entered the stately courtroom to take my place at the plaintiff's table. I was dressed in a navy pinstripe tailored business suit, crisp white blouse, and minimum accessories. Seated alongside me were my lawyers—Randy, my independent lawyer from Atlanta, and David along with Nineveh Alkhas from my Chicago law firm. Our table was off to the left and closest to the jury box. At the front of the room, a bit to the right, was the judge's bench. On the far right was the defendant's table.

David would deliver the opening statement for us. His style was pure no-nonsense to-the-point Chicago, including his animated, rapid, and direct delivery. He was a straightforward, matter-of-fact man in his late 40s who displayed a strong sense of urgency. And he was exceptionally convincing.

Seated at the defendants table were two of VeriFone/Hypercom's lawyers—Charles (Charlie) Wayne and Victoria Bruno from the Washington, DC office of the global law firm DLA Piper. This firm is a Goliath, with over 4,000 lawyers located in more than 30 countries, totally unlike the smaller firms that I was able to afford. Charlie would give the defendant's opening statement. He reminded me of a little Napoleon—short and slim with stiff, extremely erect posture and a deliberate, purposeful, slow-paced stride. He was in his 50s and had a very detached style. He wore an extremely somber expression. His small face was gaunt with a thin, pointed nose; his dark eyes were piercing and seemed to roll upward whenever he started talking. Personally, I found him to be quite arrogant and indifferent. I wondered how well he would connect with the jury.

The magistrate judge was Russell G. Vineyard, a slim man with a charming southern accent who stood at 6 foot 4 (or more) and made a commanding presence. I later joked to my lawyers that with his name being Vineyard, perhaps that was a good omen for me since I had been collecting fine wines for years and had become known by our circle of friends to be quite the wine connoisseur.

As the judge entered the chamber he was dressed in the traditional long black robe and greeted us all very cordially, yet businesslike.

"Please be seated," he said as the formality began. After confirming who would be delivering opening statements and verifying some preliminary details he called in the jury.

Earlier, when the jury had been selected, I was fascinated with the whole process. I had no idea how it worked. We needed eight jurors and two alternates. Twenty-five people were brought in and seated. Because this was a federal court the prospective jurors came from more than Atlanta proper; they were from all surrounding towns. This gave us a nice pool of white-collar workers to select from for our side, which we felt was important given the business aspects of the case.

The judge began by asking them a series of questions, and then lawyers from each side asked their questions. My lawyers handed me a scorecard of sorts to make notes on and to individually rate each one from my perspective. Some of the potential jurors were quickly dismissed if the judge felt their answers might prevent them from being unbiased. Two individuals stood out to me—in particular, one woman who was seated in the front row. She was a doctor and sort of made our case before the trial even began. She stood up and spoke of having been a victim herself of discrimination, that she knew it was real and would no doubt rule in my favor due to her own experiences. As you can imagine, she was dismissed—she was definitely not unbiased. But all the other prospective jurors heard everything she had to say.

The other individual that I remember vividly was a retired man whose wife was an executive at one of the big box retailers. My lawyers and I had a big debate about him. I figured that his wife, given her senior position, most likely shared some of the same issues that I had dealt with during her own career path, issues that her husband would have been acutely aware of. I thought he could be a great asset. My lawyers didn't agree. Eventually I won out and we picked him. He was ultimately chosen as the jury foreman.

|||||||||||

The judge now addressed the jury and explained that they were about to hear opening statements:

"I caution you that the statements that the attorneys are about to make to you are not to be considered by you as evidence in the case or instructions of the law. Nevertheless, what they have to say to you is important because it may help you understand the evidence as it is presented and the issues in this case, as well as the positions taken by the parties. So, I ask you now to give the attorneys your full attention as they address you for their opening statements."

David went first. He described my background and the career path that had brought me to being the highest-ranking woman at Hypercom. He laid the groundwork for commissions I had earned but had not been paid, and introduced the jury to the fact that everything changed for me once Philippe Tartavull was brought in to lead the company. He detailed specifics of what Philippe had done to discriminate against me over a ten-month period of time. And he established why and when I left the company as well as why I had brought this suit against Hypercom. He told them about the lawsuit that Hypercom had filed against me once I left and that they also sued my employer and two former Hypercom employees who had been hired by Ingenico. He also pointed out that although the suits were eventually dropped "the damage was done to Lisa."

He ended his opening statement by saying: *"This is a story about a bully, a CEO who thought he could treat Lisa badly because she was a woman. You will certainly hear from Lisa in detail about this. All we ask is that you listen carefully. Listen carefully to the evidence and make this situation right. Thank you."*

| | | | | | | | | | |

The defense tried to make my whole plight seem frivolous, as if I simply couldn't accept change.

"This is a case about change," Charlie Wayne began. *"More specifically, it's a case about how some people don't like to change. Lisa Shipley didn't like change and she didn't like Philippe Tartavull, but there is absolutely no evidence that Mr. Tartavull discriminated against Ms. Shipley because she was a woman."*

He went on to explain that Hypercom's board of directors had brought Philippe in because change was needed as the company was in a distant third place against its competitors. *"The board of directors decided that something had to be done,"* he emphasized. So, he continued, the board gave Philippe the authority to run the company on a day-to-day basis and they wanted him to increase profits and decrease expenses. A culture of "entitlement" had been created he told the jury, and that culture needed to be changed to a culture of accountability and performance and that's what Philippe had done.

"Now, Mr. Tartavull's new approach caused friction between him and the managing directors," Charlie admitted. But, he suggested, those changes impacted everyone, not just me. He then went into a whole dialogue about commissions and tried to establish that peers of mine, with my same title, had different responsibilities and were paid in different currency, thus not everyone could be compensated the same. I, of course, knew this was not the truth.

Eventually he addressed the issue of my complaining about Philippe, inferring I had an ulterior motive.

"Now, did Ms. Shipley complain about Mr. Tartavull? Sure. All the time. Did she ever say, he's discriminating against me because I'm a woman? Never. So what happened? As the saying goes, Ms. Shipley voted with her feet. At the end she left Hypercom.

"She had signed no agreement with Hypercom that prevented her from

going to work for a competitor. Now, given all these facts, it came as a great surprise to Hypercom when Ms. Shipley in June 2008, six months after her resignation, filed a charge of gender discrimination against Hypercom with the Federal Agency called the Equal Employment Opportunity Commission."

At the end of his opening statement Charlie referred to an email that I had sent to O.B. (my boss at the time), commenting on a press report detailing the lucrative payout of an ousted Hypercom executive that said in part, "I wish I could resign and get paid for it." Taking that email and trying to use it against me, Charlie's final comments were:

"That's why this lawsuit was filed. It was not filed because Hypercom supposedly discriminated against Ms. Shipley because she's a woman. After you have heard all the evidence I will have an opportunity to speak with you again, and at that time I will ask you to return a verdict for Hypercom. Thank you."

With that, the scene was set and testimony was about to begin. But before anyone was called to testify it was decided that in order not to influence the testimony of any other witnesses, anyone in the courtroom who would later be a witness should remain outside the courtroom so they would not be able to hear others' testimony. The only exceptions were any witnesses who were seated at the counsel table—and that would include me. At that point I handed a sticky note to my lawyers to point out that Douglas Reich, a former Hypercom lawyer who was scheduled to testify later in the trial, was sitting in the courtroom. David called it to the attention of the judge, who subsequently ordered Douglas Reich to leave the courtroom. I thought to myself, isn't that just like Hypercom— thinking that no one would notice that their former in-house lawyer had tried to blend in with regular courtroom visitors so he could get first-hand information to feed to their witnesses. How devious. And how scary.

||||||||||

While David had given the opening statement for our side, Randy would question the first witnesses.

Randy is a 6 foot 5 or 6 sandy-haired young man in his 40s with what most would call an almost baby-face cuteness, the kind of nice, respectful, southern boy look that just makes you want to mother him. He tends to wear his feelings on his sleeve, and while most of the time he expresses great warmth and sensitivity, when he gets very angry and may not verbally show it, his face gets very flushed and red. I doubt he has a mean bone in his body, but you wouldn't want to underestimate his somewhat laid-back, respectful approach. And, when it comes to being prepared he's a real perfectionist—like a hound dog with a bone. I knew he was absolutely ready for this first day of testimony from our witnesses, the first being O.B.

O.B. was my boss at Hypercom, although for much of the time I was in a management role and reported directly to the president and CEO. Here's why.

I had worked with O.B. in the mid-1990s when I was in the banking industry, and in 1995 we were married. We ended up divorcing five years later. At the time of our divorce, I had been working for Hypercom for several years. O.B. had moved on to a dot-com business, and despite our past personal relationship, we remained friends. So, when the dot-com bubble burst, I introduced him to my boss at Hypercom, who eventually hired him. Because we had developed what I would describe as an amiable and professional relationship, it all worked out just fine.

As time went on, O.B.'s roles changed, and by the time Philippe came on board, he had been promoted to a position where all the general managers of the different regions reported to him. Thus, once I was promoted I too reported to him. Despite our previous personal relationship we worked together without conflict, and no one in the company ever saw our previous relationship as a problem. Perhaps when Philippe came on board he saw things differently. Although the situation was never addressed, I suspect it may be why Philippe eventually fired O.B.

Fast-forward for a moment. O.B. found a new job after Philippe fired him and I had left Hypercom after my year of hell under Philippe's leadership. I had taken a position at Ingenico and later filed my lawsuit. In the midst of all the turmoil the one person who could totally relate to what I was going through was O.B.; no one knew the circumstances or me better than he did. As a result, he became my shoulder to cry on, my confidant, and probably the only one who could help me see the bright side from time to time. So, I guess it was no accident that eventually we realized how important we were to each another and recognized that the deep emotions that had once drawn us together were again rekindled.

Without revealing it to anyone—not our families, the kids, our friends, anyone—on August 7, 2008, eight months after I had left Hypercom, O.B. and I secretly remarried. Now it was out in the open, and hopefully the jury would be able to separate the man who was now my husband from the man who was very much a professional and had once been my boss.

I was naturally nervous for O.B. when he took the stand. I knew he was not a personal fan of Philippe. He had experienced his own problems with him and knew him well. And after constantly trying to get Philippe to make things right with me, Philippe instead found his own way to fire him. I also knew that O.B. was extremely professional, polished, and well spoken and, most important, honest.

Randy first took O.B. through a series of questions that defined his various roles before, during, and after Hypercom. Early into the testimony Randy approached the marriage situation.

"Let me back up a little bit and ask you. How long have you known Lisa Shipley?" he asked.

"I've known Lisa since about 1992," O.B. responded.

O.B. explained that he had first met me when we had worked together at Nations Bank.

"And I understand at some point in time you were married?" Randy asked.

"We were. We got married. And dates are elusive for me, but somewhere around 1995 we were married."

"And then later you were divorced?"

"We were divorced in 2000 and remarried again in 2008. That's a story in itself," he said in jest.

Randy went on to confirm that between 2000 and 2007 both O.B. and I were working for Hypercom, but that I had actually worked there about five years before O.B. had been hired.

"During that period of time from 2000 to 2007, were you ever responsible for supervising Lisa's work?" Randy asked.

O.B. responded, *"Yes, sir, I was. When I first came to work for the company Lisa worked in the U.S. Sales Division and I supervised her work, but did not supervise her directly. She reported to the CEO of the company to create some separateness between us and her."*

Randy then questioned O.B. about my performance.

"She was a superstar. We were a growing company in the industry. She developed relationships with First Data Corporation, grew the business significantly well, won a lot of sales awards for being the highest revenue producer in the company." He went on to confirm that he had recommended me for the promotion to managing director of North America because of my performance and noted that the approval came from the CEO.

There then ensued conversation about the equality of all the people who held the same position that I did. He explained it organizationally, saying they were all on the same line. He confirmed that all managing directors were direct reports to him but were general managers of their own lines of business.

O.B. explained that during his tenure with the company he worked for four different CEOs and that the same structures stayed in place the whole time; that is, the managing director's positions were essentially the same.

The next vein of questioning touched on a very important aspect.

"Was it common for managing directors to visit their clients with the CEO or president of the company?" Randy asked.

"Yes sir. I mean, very much so. I mean, maintaining customer relationships, developing a pipeline and a prospect channel was the—one of the most important aspects of that role."

"Was that important for the managing director to get that support from the president?" Randy probed.

"Absolutely. It's comfortable for our prospects and for our customers to see the senior person in the company. You know, it builds confidence in a company as a supplier to our customers."

A few minutes later Randy asked, *"When Philippe Tartavull came over as president did you travel with him to visit customers?"*

"Not in North America," O.B. clarified.

"Where did you travel?"

"We traveled to Mexico and Brazil together."

"Did he ever travel to visit customers with Lisa Shipley?"

"Not that I'm aware of."

O.B.'s testimony substantiated one of my strongest complaints that while Philippe flew around the world to visit other customers, he refused to go with me to any of mine, even though my customers generated the greatest revenues. Then there was the issue of Philippe not allowing me to go to the Cartes trade show in Paris. Randy hit that issue next.

"Can you tell us a little bit about a trade show by the name of Cartes?"

O.B. explained, *"Cartes is the largest European or international trade show for the whole credit card business, both issuing and acquiring. It's a little different than most trade shows in the world because all of our customers globally show up at Cartes. It's a pretty important venue to meet and entertain customers."*

"When you were in the role of managing director or similar role for North America was it common for you to travel to attend the Cartes trade show?" Randy asked.

"When I was the general manager of the International Sales I traveled to attend Cartes, you know, every year."

"Was it common at Cartes to have business planning meetings among the other managing directors?" asked Randy.

"Well, anytime we would get the general managers together we had business planning meetings to have discussions about our next year. Cartes occurs every year in late November or early December, and so it's a good time to wrap up the current year and then to plan for the next year."

For nearly all of the next hour or so the questions focused on compensation, with Randy questioning O.B. about the compensation structure for the four other managing directors compared to mine. He clarified each one's duties to demonstrate that all five of us were accountable for the same activities as well as covering how compensation and bonuses had been paid. Detailed charts and documents were shown, all leading up to the fact that I had been unable to get a compensation plan approved from Philippe, and thus had not been paid any commissions as a managing director for months after taking over the new role.

By now it was late afternoon and a 15-minute break was called. I hoped the break would refresh the jury because this detailed financial discussion had to be wearing on them. Yet, I knew it was critical testimony of my being treated differently from the men who were my peers.

|||||||||||

When the jury returned, testimony resumed with a discussion about my compensation plan. O.B. expressed his frustration at not being able to resolve the issue for me.

"Philippe Tartavull took an interest in her compensation plan and wanted to craft it himself. In fact he said that he would take the responsibility for the development of the plan."

"Did he develop the plan right away?" Randy asked.

"No, he did not. We had a series of exchanges about the development plan. He told me not to worry, it was in his court."

It was only natural to question whether the other managing directors had trouble getting their compensation plans finalized in this time period. O.B. made the difference clear.

"No sir. They were all done and solidified earlier in the year."

Shortly thereafter O.B. pointed out why not having a compensation plan impacted my ability to maximize doing my job.

"It's extremely difficult. A compensation plan is a road map," he explained.

Randy then questioned O.B. about the plan under which I had been paid during the period I was waiting to get my new compensation plan finalized. Did he know that it was lower than other managing directors? If so, had he talked to Philippe about it not being equal to my peers? And if so, what was Philippe's reaction?

"Philippe said we gave her a $50,000 increase. She should be happy."

"Without regard to whether she was paid the same?" Randy asked.

"Right."

In other words, unlike all of my peers, I should have been happy simply to be given a raise when I was promoted. That right there was a pretty good indication of Philippe's differential treatment.

Randy then asked whether I had been paid any commission in April when commission would ordinarily be expected, particularly since there was no new plan in place for me.

"Not for her new role," he responded. *"We couldn't pay her. There was no plan."*

O.B. later confirmed that even once a plan was put in place, my payments were delayed. *"In fact several of her incentive payments were late or held up while Philippe and Clint Jones* [Hypercom's chief of staff] *decided, you know, how we would pay."*

"To the best of my recollection everyone else was paid timely," he later added.

Aside from the compensation issue, the different way Philippe treated me was also at stake, so Randy asked O.B., *"Can you describe for us some of your observations of the way he treated her?"*

"Philippe was dismissive toward Lisa," O.B. testified. *"She asked him to travel on several occasions to see customers. He wouldn't go. He was disrespectful to her in front of her peers in management meetings and in other circumstances of work.*

"We had a building next door that was called a networking building. We had a meeting over there one day and as we were doing business reviews, and all of the general managers from around the world were in this room, Lisa was giving her presentation about some business solutions and Philippe interrupted her several times, left the building—during her presentation."

"Just walked out? No excuse, just left?" Randy asked.

"I'm not sure how long he was gone, but he came back after Lisa's presentation was over."

Randy asked, *"Did you get a sense that he was treating her differently because she was a woman?"*

"I did get that sense," O.B. responded.

With that, Hypercom's lawyer, Charlie Wayne, objected, and the court sustained. Randy rephrased the question and O.B. answered again. Again Charlie objected. Once again the court sustained. So Randy rephrased his question once more.

"When you saw Mr. Tartavull, Philippe, treating her in this way, how did that affect her standing as a managing director in comparison to her peers?"

"In work environments as you work with your associates and with your peers, you know, respect is important. And to be disrespected by the CEO of the company is not seen to be appropriate," O.B. explained.

When asked if I ever complained to him about the way Philippe treated me, O.B. responded: *"She did. She complained fairly often about his behavior. She didn't like being disrespected. She didn't understand why he was treating her differently as compared to her peers in the other regions. She was the largest producer of revenue for the company. She didn't understand his attitude or his disrespect toward her."*

Randy followed up by asking if O.B. took those concerns to anyone.

"I did. I talked to Philippe. He was very dismissive to me about it. You know, it's not important. We gave her a pay raise. She should be happy. Those kind of comments."

Randy then questioned whether he had taken my concerns to Human Resources and O.B. explained that at the time there was no human resources manager, that the last one had left in 2006, and so he took it to the CEO, which was at the time the appropriate thing to do.

"Did Philippe deny that he was treating Ms. Shipley differently?" Randy asked.

"No. His comments were more dismissive. He just said, I don't know what she's worrying about. He would just shoo me away when I would have these kinds of conversations with him. And, it was my role as her manager and the manager of all the managing directors to be the advocate to the company. That was my role.

"I was pretty powerless in my effort to change things."

| | | | | | | | | | |

The testimony next turned to discussion about the multiple lawsuits that Hypercom filed more than a year after I left and while I was working for Ingenico, lawsuits in which they sued me personally as well as the two former employees Ingenico had hired. Randy questioned O.B. as to how he believed those suits impacted me:

"I saw an extremely powerful and confident person lose confidence, lose trust in her personal abilities to be successful. I saw her become embarrassed. I saw her have hurt feelings. I saw just a different person evolve from the attacks.

"She was worried about her future, her ability to perform, to be employable in the world. She spent a great number of years developing her reputation as one of the most successful salespeople in the industry and to be attacked by a former employer was for her a personally discouraging and disruptive time in her life. She was a superstar in the industry. That was debased and demeaned by a meaningless lawsuit."

Noting that the lawsuits were eventually dropped, Randy went on to query whether those reactions went away after a few weeks.

Again, Charlie objected. But this time the judge overruled, so O.B. responded:

"Her confidence did not and has not returned to its complete level. She's been distraught; she's still been questioning what she did wrong. So she was a person of significant power and influence who began to doubt herself significantly."

Wanting to demonstrate the long-term impact on me of that lawsuit, Randy then asked: *"We talked about Ms. Shipley's reaction to the lawsuits that were filed against her. Have you been able to observe Ms. Shipley today? And can you tell us a little bit—any thoughts about her reaction to the discrimination that she feels like she endured under Mr. Tartavull and how she reacted to that?"*

Charlie immediately objected. *"We've been over this,"* he said, trying to derail an answer. But it didn't work.

"I don't believe so on this particular point," the judge responded. *"I'll overrule the objection."*

O.B. went on to answer and his final comments pretty much summed up what I had endured then and even to that very day:

"Lisa was very disappointed that Hypercom chose to attack her. She gave the company prime years of her life as a salesperson. She was a great performer during her time there and so to be attacked affected her personally. As I stated, it did destroy her confidence. It caused her concerns with her health—heart palpitations—other [things], *lack of sleep, just a series of additional stresses and worries that we normally don't have to deal with."*

With that, Randy concluded his questions. Next, Charlie Wayne would begin his cross-examination.

- 9 -

LOST IN DETAILS

VeriFone/Hypercom's Washington, DC lawyer, Charlie, was now up. I wondered how the jury would relate to Charlie. To me, he acted rather arrogant, like he was smarter than my team of lawyers. I had only shaken his hand once, and that was the first time we met. As the days would go on, neither one of us acknowledged the other. He would shake hands with David or Nineveh but, strange to me, would never shake Randy's hand. I always felt that it burned him that my unknown, sole practicing Atlanta lawyer had taken him to task and had made it this far. Now it was his turn and I expected him to be pretty aggressive with his questioning of O.B.

Early into Charlie's cross-examination he posed a question about the three-year period prior to Philippe being put in the leadership role as president. *"That was a tumultuous period of time for the company, was it not?"*

O.B. characterized it as "pretty erratic" but Charlie pressed for "tumultuous," asking, *"You'd agree with the word 'tumultuous,' would you not?"*

"I don't know if 'tumultuous' was the right word," O.B. challenged. *"But it was a hard time for the company."*

Charlie took that to mean there was a lot of disruption and O.B. agreed. Charlie asked, *"Because there were no fewer than four chief executive officers during that period of time, correct?"* Charlie then went on to name each of the four leaders and who each was replaced by leading up to the time that Philippe was brought in.

"And one of the effects of all this fluctuation and this disruption was the compensation plans for various employees were delayed in becoming effective, correct?" Charlie asked, trying to establish that delaying my compensation plan was nothing personal, rather it was just timing.

O.B. disagreed. *"Not that I can remember dramatically."* Again, Charlie pressed, wanting to infer that I wasn't the only one affected by the change in leadership. But O.B. did not budge in his disagreement, saying: *"I'm not trying to be argumentative, but which change in leadership and at what time? I mean, it is possible that some plans could have been delayed for certain people over time. I mean, that happens. People change roles a lot, so I'll try to be more specific if you can point me to the right direction."*

Seeming determined to get the answer he wanted, Charlie then challenged O.B. by referencing various pages of his deposition. But that only seemed to confuse the issue more. He also laboriously went over everything that O.B. had said in his deposition about my promotion, even detailed all the variables of what eventually had become my compensation plan.

I'm not sure any of the back-and-forth debating was anything but confusing to the jury. Quite frankly, it was even confusing to me and it was my situation they were talking about.

Charlie then tried to infer that it was my fault that Philippe never visited any of my customers by bringing into evidence an email that Philippe had sent to all managing directors and O.B. six months after assuming the president's role. In part Philippe said in the email: "I am sure by now you have made good contacts with all our major clients. I would like to take this opportunity to call our three or four top customers and distributors in this region. I would appreciate it if you would send me the list of those with the contact name."

Charlie followed this up by reading an email that I had written to O.B. the day after Philippe's email in which I wrote, "This is a bad idea. He's hard enough to understand in person much less on the phone." To which O.B. replied, *"For the record, I agree."*

Charlie asked O.B. if he had in fact agreed with me and he confirmed that he had. Charlie then tried to use this comment to demonstrate how O.B. personally felt about Philippe.

"Now, you did not like Mr. Tartavull's management style, correct?" he asked.

"I didn't agree with everything he did. He was difficult. He was hard to understand. He didn't show very well with employees or our customers," O.B. stated.

Charlie took that answer to imply that O.B. believed that Philippe simply didn't treat any employee well, but O.B. quickly clarified that. *"He wasn't nasty to everybody, if that's what you're saying. He had his moments."*

Clearly, Charlie was doing everything he could to discount the fact that Philippe treated me any differently from anyone else, but O.B. wasn't allowing it so Charlie moved to another topic.

"Now, let's talk about you testified that Ms. Shipley told you that she thought that Mr. Tartavull was treating her—was discriminating against her because she was a woman. As a senior executive of Hypercom you were familiar with the Employee Handbook, were you not?" Charlie questioned.

O.B. confirmed that he was familiar with it.

"Now you say that you told Mr. Tartavull that Ms. Shipley complained to you that he was discriminating against her because she was a woman. Do I have that correct?" Charlie went on. O.B. agreed that Charlie had it correct.

"But you never reported it to Human Resources, correct?"

"No, sir, we didn't have a human resources manager," O.B. pointed out.

Charlie then asked if he had reported it to Mr. Keiper, the CEO at the time, and O.B. noted that the CEO and he had numerous conversations about Philippe and his management style and his treatment of Lisa.

Charlie seemed to get quite frustrated, and the more frustrated he became, the more tense things got.

"That's not my question," Charlie said defiantly. *"I'm asking who you told who was higher in the organization than you that Ms. Shipley was being discriminated against because she was a woman, not that Mr. Tartavull might have been hard on her, whatever—however you want to say it, but she was being treated differently because she was a woman. You told no one, correct?"*

"I told Mr. Keiper," O.B. reminded Charlie. *"We had conversations about Philippe and about the role that he was playing and his style."*

"Are you telling us that you told Mr. Keiper that Ms. Shipley was making a claim of gender discrimination against Mr. Tartavull and thus against the company. Is that what you're telling us?" Charlie somewhat angrily challenged.

"No, that's not what I said, sir," O.B. replied calmly.

"Okay. Thank you. You never reported Ms. Shipley's allegation of gender discrimination to Doug Reich, the general counsel, the head lawyer, did you?"

O.B. confirmed that he had not gone to the general counsel.

Charlie went on to make it sound like O.B. had done nothing to generate an investigation; he had not reported to Human Resources and had not notified the general counsel. He then ended his cross-examination, obviously hoping that at this point it would seem to the jury that O.B. had not adequately reported discrimination. But Randy quickly asked to redirect and confirmed from O.B. that he had in fact talked to an in-house counsel about the discrimination. He also had O.B. point out that the counsel reported to the general counsel, a perfectly appropriate process for handling the situation. He then revisited the "tumultuous" period of time and asked O.B. if during that time anyone else's compensation plan was delayed. "No sir," O.B. responded, once again confirming that Philippe had treated my compensation plan differently.

When Randy ended his redirect, Charlie requested a brief re-cross-examination in order to revisit the issue of O.B. speaking with the Hypercom lawyer.

"And in your mind when you were talking to him about that [Lisa's compensation], *did that relate to her claim that she was being treated differently because of her gender?"* Charlie asked.

"Yes, we talked about Lisa's compensation. We talked about her complaints, you know, about Philippe. And I don't know where you're headed specifically, but we had lots of discussions about this situation," O.B. responded.

"Are you telling us that you told Mr. Ivezaj [the Hypercom lawyer] *that Ms. Shipley felt that she was being discriminated against by Mr. Tartavull because she was a woman?"* Charlie asked in a disbelieving tone.

"Yes," O.B. affirmed, making it clear that he had indeed discussed the issue of discrimination.

That was not an answer Charlie expected and he had no more questions.

With that, O.B. was excused. I thought O.B. did a much better job on the stand than he had done in his depositions. I was proud of him for doing so well. But I was also sad that he couldn't be sitting right next to me as I endured the rest of the trial.

|| || || || ||

It was getting late in the day but there was time to call one more witness—Chris Alexander, a former chairman, CEO, and president of Hypercom. David, my Chicago lawyer, conducted the examination.

Chris confirmed that he had been chairman, CEO, and president from 2000 to 2005 and said that during that period, *"There wasn't anything I wasn't responsible for."*

David asked about the duties of managing directors or general managers, confirming that they were one in the same job. He then asked Chris to explain the duties of the job.

"Well, their primary responsibilities involved revenue generation which would be sales, gross margin management, expense management, all operations as they related to that particular region and localization of research and development."

The defense objected to David's line of questioning, arguing that since Chris had left the company in 2005, many things could have changed and his experience was not relevant to the time period in question. But David argued that Chris's testimony was indeed relevant and that his testimony went to the credibility of our case that these jobs in fact are the same and that they historically have been and haven't changed.

The court agreed and overruled the defense's objection.

During Chris's testimony he was asked to verify not only the sameness of duties of all managing directors but whether he, in his position, visited customers and how compensation was treated. But the latter two issues were objected to and the court sustained the objections. Chris was, however, able to answer questions about what he thought about my performance.

"During the time that you worked with her did you have an opinion of her as an employee at Hypercom?" David asked.

"Yes, I did. She was in my entire work experience one of the two best account managers that I have ever seen," Chris began.

"There's more to selling and managing an account than simply going in, getting the order, and then coming back to the customer when he needs more product. She went the extra mile. She provided training, assistance to the customer. If the customer needed anything, she was right there. As a result of this extra effort, I think it led us to a higher sales achievement than we would have through a salesman who simply went in, picked up the order, said thank you very much, took the customer to lunch, and came back when he thought the customer would be out of product."

Chris was then asked about an award named Mover and Shaker for which he had nominated me. He was asked to explain what factors led him to nominate me.

In part Chris explained: *"She was asked by me personally to start up a new sales division for the company, independent sales organization. Up to that point we had not tried to sell into that particular channel. She accepted that job frankly with very little resources. She was incredibly successful in that particular activity and, frankly, at some personal difficulties to herself. She had three kids. And the travel involved in what I was asking her to do was substantially more than what she was experiencing as the account manager on one of our very largest accounts. So as a result of her abilities and, frankly, her personal sacrifice, I thought that she would be well-recognized as a mover and shaker for that particular publication."*

Chris's explanation was a nice ending to substantiate that I had not only performed well in my role but also had excelled. Apparently, Charlie felt there was little to gain by doing any cross-examination because when asked by the court if he had any cross-examination he responded, *"No questions, Your Honor."*

It was very late in the day and the court suggested that since our next witness would likely take longer than 15 minutes we should adjourn until the next morning. For our team, it would not be the end of the day though. We had all agreed that it would be best to stay in the same downtown hotel for the duration of the trial, so I had checked in Sunday, the night before the trial began. After leaving court, we all went to dinner and returned to David's suite to prepare for the next day.

It was very late when I went to my room. I was tired and feeling mentally exhausted, yet instead of immediately falling to sleep I laid in the dark, my mind racing, wondering what drama there might be the next day when Bernie and Greg would be witnesses. No doubt they would be put on the hot seat by the defense for leaving Hypercom and following me to Ingenico. And there would be all those questions about Hypercom's suit against each of them personally. Yes, tomorrow could be another very intense and exhausting day.

- 10 -

THE CONSPIRACY
THAT WASN'T

I had mixed feelings as day two started. I was humbled that some of the people I had worked with at Hypercom and others were willing to come to Atlanta, just to testify on my behalf. But my nerves were also on edge because depending on how much time testimony took with all the witnesses, I could be taking the stand myself in the afternoon. I knew I couldn't let my nerves take over—I couldn't blow it. I had spent four years to get to this day. I had earlier researched over-the-counter drugs for anxiety and found something called Relacore. I decided to try it way back when I had taken my deposition and it seemed to help me keep my stress manageable—at least I believed it did. So, I decided to take it again. Every four hours I would take a pill and it seemed to calm my nerves.

Among former colleagues who were testifying were Greg and Bernie. They had already been through their own pain and distress months earlier when Hypercom had sued each of them personally for going to work at Ingenico. I was still feeling guilty and responsible for the anguish they had been put through.

Also scheduled to testify were Ed Labry, my current boss and president of First Data Corporation, Hypercom's largest client, as well as my former boss, Chris Justice, president of Ingenico.

Then there was Jaime Arroyo who flew from Mexico City on his own dime just to testify on my behalf. Jaime had been one of my peers. Although he was no longer employed by Hypercom, he had been vice president and managing director for Mexico, the Caribbean, and the Central American countries during the time that I had the same position for North America. Jaime was first to take the witness stand.

Nineveh Alkhas, the third member of my legal team, handled his direct examination. She began by establishing that Jaime and I had been peers at Hypercom and asked, *"Are you here on your own volition today or were you court-ordered?"*

Jaime confirmed that he was here of his own free will.

"Are you being paid for your testimony today," she then asked. *"Not at all,"* Jaime responded.

"Ms. Shipley's not reimbursing you for your time here? And is anybody paying for your airfare or accommodations?"

Again, he emphasized "no," making it clear that he was here at his own cost because he wanted to be here.

Next Jaime was asked to detail the duties of his role. He explained that while language and some country laws differed, those aspects of his job were not significant and that the primary duties were the same for all managing directors.

He was then asked if Philippe had visited any of his customers. *"All of them but one,"* he responded, and one by one he named them.

"Did you ask Mr. Tartavull to accompany you to visit these clients or did he ask to visit them?" Nineveh inquired.

"I did not. He asked me," Jaime explained.

Continuing on that subject, Jaime was asked if Philippe's presence at these companies helped him do his job. *"Yes, of course. It's very important for the president of the company to accompany you and go with you to visit the president of a bank. It gives you one more opportunity to talk to the customer, to talk to the high end—the decision maker of that particular bank.”*

It was important for the jury to hear how important it was to have the president call on clients. It would help them see how detrimental it was to me that Philippe refused to visit any of my clients.

Nineveh then moved her questioning to the topic of meetings that the managing directors had with Philippe.

“Did you make any observations during those meetings about Mr. Tartavull's treatment towards Ms. Shipley?” she asked.

“Yes. It was in every single meeting he was asking more questions to Lisa. He was persistent and insisting on asking questions. But the difference is that those questions were not constructive—was just asking questions in a destructive way, just asking this and that and that and that so without a focus or a final goal.

“It was destructive. The other managing directors would have the opportunity to feel him as more productive in trying to build a team and trying to help you, support you in your endeavor of sales or managing.”

“Did you find Mr. Tartavull's questions of Lisa in particular to be supportive of Ms. Shipley?” she asked.

“It was not. It was destructive,” Jaime said.

Nineveh then asked if he recalled any other incidents.

“One actually sticks in my mind,” he began. *“I was surprised because one day we were all reporting and Lisa used to be the first one because he asked. So—and one particular meeting Lisa started reporting, you know, doing her presentation, and all of a sudden he just asked maybe one or two questions, stood up and left. Never came back—well, never came back during the presentation. He came back one hour later.”*

“Did you find this unusual that Mr. Tartavull would just walk out during Ms. Shipley's presentation?” Nineveh asked.

“Very unusual because even he sometimes had to walk away for a call or something like that, he said, hold on, Jaime. I'll be right back. And we had to all stop until he came back, and this time it didn't happen.”

To further emphasize how I had been treated differently Nineveh asked one last question about this incident. *"Did Mr. Tartavull ever walk out in the middle of any of the other managing directors' presentations like he did when Ms. Shipley presented?"*

"No. He did not!" Jaime confirmed.

The questioning then turned to the Cartes trade show in Paris—the one Philippe had refused to let me attend.

Jaime pointed out that Cartes was the biggest show in the world for the industry and that the show was attended by all the managing directors and about five managers from some of the business units. *"But,"* he added, *"Lisa was not there."* He went on to elaborate about how the show provided a very good opportunity to talk to customers and find out what they expected for the next year. *"You have an idea of the forecast for what they want for next year,"* he pointed out. *"And you have opportunity to show them the product specific for that need."*

Jaime also explained that on the last day of the show Philippe held a strategy meeting where each managing director had a turn to present their sales for the quarter and project what they thought was going to happen the next year. It was in essence a quarterly meeting. *"I had an opportunity to talk to different customers so I knew exactly what I needed for the next year, so I had a certain idea of what my forecast looked like or what my budget would look like for the next year. For example, I got a prospect I was pursuing for a long time."*

Jaime's testimony again pointed out opportunities I had missed by not being allowed to attend the show. When Jaime was asked if he thought it was unusual that I was absent, he responded, *"Very unusual, because usually she was at every single show like everybody—like every other managing director."*

Wrapping up her questioning Nineveh asked Jaime if he was surprised when I resigned from Hypercom.

"That's a two-sided question," Jaime said. *"I was surprised because Lisa was a very good performer. She always out-performed me. It was a healthy*

competition, let's put it that way. So I was very surprised because you don't let somebody of that caliber or that high production stamina leave the company. I was not surprised because of the way she was treated, so I would do the same and look for some other opportunity."

I was so impressed with Jaime's candor—his absolute resolve to tell the truth. As I watched the jury, they appeared to be very focused on everything he had to say. Hopefully that was a good sign. It would be interesting to see how the defense would try to twist everything around.

|||||||||

Charlie hit hard as he began his cross-examination. *"In May of 2009, you were fired from your job at Hypercom, right?"*

Jaime admitted he had been let go after receiving a call saying he was no longer needed because supposedly his position no longer existed, but you could tell he was offended at the inference that for some reason he had been fired. But, Charlie continued to make it sound like Jaime wasn't performing up to par by implying the reason he had been let go was because his numbers were not satisfactory.

"No," Jaime firmly stated.

"Oh, you're sure?" Charlie somewhat sarcastically questioned.

"I am sure," Jaime insisted.

Charlie abruptly changed the subject moving to questions about the Cartes trade show.

"Now, you did not ask to be excused from attending the Cartes trade show in Paris in November of 2007, did you?"

Jaime seemed confused by the question and never did really respond in a way that I suspect Charlie was hoping for. I think Jaime didn't understand why he was being asked the question, but I knew. It was Charlie's roundabout way of eventually asking Jaime if he was aware that I had asked not to go to the Carte trade show. Jaime, probably still a bit confused with the line of questioning, admitted he knew nothing about my having asked that. The line of questioning, however, allowed Charlie to say, *"In fact you're not aware that not only did she ask not to go to the trade show, but she went on vacation to the Cayman Islands instead? You're not aware of that, are you?"* To which Jaime replied, *"No. I am not."*

Cleverly, Charlie had found a way to use a question to drop in incomplete information that he apparently thought would be damaging to me. Then he abruptly changed the subject. What was never allowed to be clarified was that although I had actually gone on vacation at the time of the Cartes show, I only did so after coming to the realization that I would not be allowed to go to Cartes, regardless of the number of times I asked. With all of my peers and customers at the show, I knew it would be a good opportunity to take my vacation time—I also desperately needed a break from the stress I had been going through. I later was able to explain this when I testified. For now though, I could only hope that the whole line of questioning was as confusing to the jury as it seemed to be to Jaime.

Charlie next tried to establish that a trade show called ETA (Electronic Transactions Association) was actually the main show for my territory of the Americas. But Jaime disputed that, explaining, *"It was going down and Cartes has become much bigger."*

His response seemed to anger Charlie. *"And why don't you answer my question?"* he demanded. *"Isn't it true that in 2007 the ETA trade show was the main trade show for North America and the rest of the Americas?"*

Jaime's answer was short, firm, and to the point. *"No!"*

With that, Charlie moved on, turning his attention to Philippe and his demeanor, trying to establish that Philippe was hard on everyone, not just me.

When asked if Philippe was sometimes abrupt to every managing director, Charlie didn't like Jaime's answer. *"No, he was not hard, I mean, just with Lisa,"* Jaime said.

"Oh, really?" Charlie exclaimed. *"So he singled her out and he was not*

difficult—he was not hard on anybody else, is that your testimony?"

"Yes sir," Jaime confirmed, which ended that vein of questioning also. Shortly thereafter cross-examination ended.

|| || || || ||

Up next was Bernie Frey. Bernie being here was significant to me. Through my entire ordeal, Bernie was my key confidant. I told him everything. He was the only one I had told of my plans to leave Hypercom. After I left Hypercom, Bernie was left behind to deal with Philippe and to try to fix many of the things Philippe had blocked me from doing for my sales team. It's interesting to note here that one of my biggest fights with Philippe before leaving was about the new commission plans he was trying to introduce. They were full of huge changes and simply awful. I feared that if Philippe insisted on the changes, I would lose very good people. After I left, Bernie put forward pretty much the same argument that I had, and Philippe finally agreed to stick with the old plans that were in place. While I was pleased with the outcome, I also felt that it was just one more example of how I, a woman, couldn't be heard but a man with the same rationale got it done.

I expected that Bernie would be a great witness for me, and it would be interesting to see how the defense would try to twist his testimony during cross-examination. Bernie is honest to a fault. I don't think you could get him to lie if you tortured him. I trusted him with my life and still do to this very day. I figured the jury would feel that sense of honesty as well.

After being sworn in, Randy began direct examination by confirming with Bernie that he was currently an employee of Ingenico but had previously been employed by Hypercom, reported to me, and managed sales in the United States Banking channel.

"During the time that you worked there, what were your observations of how Lisa Shipley was performing?" Randy asked.

"Always good. I learned a lot, and she was great." Bernie said.

"Was there ever an opportunity in performing your job that you had opportunities to interact with Lisa and Philippe Tartavull together at the same time?" asked Randy.

Bernie explained that interactions had mostly been at corporate headquarters in Phoenix when there were meetings.

"Did Philippe ever travel with Lisa to visit any of the customers that you might share in common with Lisa?" Randy asked.

"I don't recall ever being in a customer meeting with Philippe and Lisa or knowing that they were at one," Bernie responded.

Randy then asked, *"Where you had an opportunity to observe Philippe Tartavull and Lisa Shipley interacting together can you tell what your observations were about how Philippe Tartavull acted towards Lisa?"*

Bernie's recollections were direct and very candid. *"I think he treated Lisa in a dismissive manner, and I guess 'disdainful' would be an appropriate word. He did not treat her well. He didn't seem to show her respect."*

"Did he seem to value her opinion?" Randy continued.

"Consistent with lack of respect and dismissiveness, I would say no."

"Were you able to observe his treatment in comparison to the other managing directors?" Randy probed.

"Yes. It was different. He was not always nice to people, but he was unpleasant in a different way to other people. When he was unpleasant it was more an active unpleasantness versus dismissive unpleasantness. During breaks he would spend his time with other managers and didn't seem to care to associate with Lisa in between the meetings and things.

"I never saw it different than that. When I noticed the behavior it was consistent."

Randy next asked Bernie how he thought this treatment impacted my ability to succeed as a manager.

Charlie immediately objected, but the court just as quickly overruled and Bernie answered.

"I'll speak for myself based on what I think," Bernie began. *"I don't think Lisa was able to properly represent my channel, and sales and operations it was*

affecting—well, yes, it had to have affected her job because it was affecting my job. Because if she wasn't being respected or listened to, then my channel wasn't getting the resources and attention it needed."

Bernie was then asked if I had ever discussed the situation with him, if I had ever told him I felt that I was being treated differently because I was a woman.

"I don't know that she actually said that it's because she's a woman. Lisa is a really tough person and she doesn't really complain much, so there wasn't a lot of that going on. But it was clear that she felt she was being treated differently and as such wasn't able to do her job."

When asked about what kind of conversations he had had with me prior to my leaving, he said, *"Basically that she felt like she had to leave and she didn't want to and it made her feel bad.*

"Lisa and I had known each other for a long time and I think there was a sense of abandonment there on her part—you know, she helped me a lot and she felt bad about leaving. It was clear that her relationship with Philippe Tartavull made her unable to do her job. It was hurting the others of us because it was trickling down and wasn't doing any of us any good.

"I felt that Lisa left because she was—it was doing a lot of us a favor and that she did things internally before leaving to try to help us. I'm sure to some degree there is, I can't do my job, and she needed to look out for herself. But, as I say, most of the time when she was talking to me it was less about her and more about what she wanted to accomplish for me and others within the company before she left."

Pressing for more insight Randy asked, *"Did she seem sad? Did she seem remorseful that she was leaving?"* To which Bernie responded, *"Yes."*

Randy then asked Bernie to explain a little more about what he meant about my trying to protect others by leaving.

"It was a challenging culture at the time and there were some compensation things that had been changed and they were not acceptable to people, a lot of people who were considering leaving. There were morale issues and some of

the things that Lisa did before she left put pieces in place that improved the situation for those she left behind," Bernie explained.

Randy asked Bernie to explain why the commission plan was so critical.

"In sales you have quotas. If you don't get to a certain percentage you got almost no compensation," Bernie began. *"In sales, half of what you earn, sometimes two-thirds of what you earn, is not your salary, it's what you earn on commissions. So the way to pay people less is to raise their quota numbers so high and don't pay them for their first 50, 60, or 70 percent of what they bring in, and if you do that, you very quickly lower their earning capabilities and things.*

"If you raise that quota so high, you can't get to your targeted earnings, which is what you kind of base your living on. And that was being manipulated. I felt it was being manipulated. Others felt it was being manipulated. And it was affecting morale and I believe it was going to affect whether the people who reported to me continued to work there."

Bernie did a great job of explaining exactly what Philippe was trying to do by changing the commission plan and how it was destroying morale. And because Philippe had been so disrespectful of me, I was unable to do anything about it.

Randy wanted to make it clear that my leaving Hypercom wasn't necessarily a move up in my career, so he asked Bernie, *"From your perspective when Lisa left the company was it for a better opportunity?"*

"No, no!" Bernie stressed. *"There are two primary companies in the U.S. in this industry and they are VeriFone and Hypercom. Those are the big leagues, if you will. Ingenico was struggling, in my channel in particular, had almost no market share and about the same level of respect, frankly, from a lot of people in the industry. I did not perceive, nor do I believe the industry would have seen that career change as a step up. On the contrary, it would have been a step down or a step backward."*

Following some discussion about Philippe eventually being permanently named CEO and president, Randy moved to the fact that

Bernie had decided to leave Hypercom and join me at Ingenico. But he had waited to resign until he received commission on a large account. Bernie was well aware of the fact that after I had left Hypercom they failed to pay me my due commission on sales that I had generated prior to leaving, so Randy asked, *"Knowing about that experience* [Lisa not getting paid], *did that impact your decisions when you went to Ingenico as well?"*

"Absolutely," Bernie confirmed. *"I chose not to resign until after I got paid for some commissions that were due me because after what I saw happen to Lisa when she resigned, I was afraid they would do the same thing for me. And my compensation plan in 2009 was unacceptable when it was given to me,"* Bernie explained, adding that his boss at the time told him that she had not even seen it and agreed that it was unacceptable and would try to improve it. *"Several months later she finally did. I was afraid that based on what I saw happen to Lisa, that if I didn't get paid first, I wouldn't get paid. So I timed my resignation accordingly."*

Randy next began to ask questions that related to the lawsuit that Hypercom had filed against both Bernie and Greg after they had resigned and moved to Ingenico. The defense continued to object until the court finally ordered Randy to be very specific with any further questions regarding this topic, no open-ended questions. There were so many objections from the defense that Bernie got confused and finally asked the court, *"Can I ask a question? Am I allowed to discuss what was in the lawsuit that was filed against me?"*

The court explained to Bernie that he was allowed to answer any question asked of him unless there was an objection, which was why he had asked Randy to be specific with the questions he asked. With that, Randy asked, *"Did you tell anyone at Hypercom when you resigned that you and Greg Boardman had planned this move to go together for a long time?"*

"No. Quite the contrary. I told all of them the exact same thing, which is that to my knowledge Greg had been recruited by Chris Justice, the president of Ingenico, to report to Chris Justice, and Greg intended to resign earlier than

me. I became aware that Greg was going to resign earlier than me and I asked that he wait.

"I asked that Greg not resign until I knew that I had gotten my commissions."

Once again the defense tried to object, but the court overruled and Bernie's response stood firm.

Bernie was then asked to look at an exhibit and identify it. The exhibit document was the lawsuit that was filed against Bernie by Hypercom after he had resigned and gone to work for Ingenico.

"When did you first receive this lawsuit?" Randy asked.

"As I recall, about a week after—everything had exploded around me," Bernie recalled nervously.

"What do you mean by everything exploded around you?" Randy asked.

Bernie began to explain. *"When I resigned I did not have a non-compete agreement. Sometime shortly thereafter* [after he had left Hypercom] *I got a call from an attorney on my cell phone who introduced himself as Hypercom's attorney and told me that there was going to be a session with a judge in Pittsburgh* [where Bernie lived at the time] *in two hours because they were filing an injunction to keep me from going to work at Ingenico, and I could be there if I wanted. I didn't even know I'd been sued yet, so I didn't make that meeting. But I called Ingenico and told them what they had said and the attorney was nice. He gave me a phone number and I gave that information to Ingenico and they found some attorneys in Pittsburgh that went and represented me and were able to stop the preliminary injunction. And then sometime, I think a few days, after I got a copy of this document."*

Things then got a little testy as Randy began to read from the lawsuit document. *"It says, upon information and belief, a former Hypercom employee named Lisa Shipley recruited both Mr. Frey and Mr. Boardman to join Ingenico and Mr. Frey and Mr. Boardman in turn recruited each other to join Ingenico in violation of their respective non-solicitation agreements.*

"Now, based on what you told me about your resignation, is this statement true?"

Immediately the defense objected, but the court overruled and Randy continued. *"Based on what you had told people at the time of your resignation, was this statement true?"*

"No," Bernie responded.

"What you had told other people was inconsistent with what this allegation is, is that correct?" Bernie was asked.

"Yes, that is correct."

Randy then read from Hypercom's allegations, which suggested that Bernie and Greg had intended to use Hypercom's trade secrets and confidential and proprietary information to entice away Hypercom's customers. Randy wanted to know if that had been Bernie and Greg's plan. Bernie, of course, denied that anything of that kind had ever been planned.

The defense continued to try to object but the court continued to overrule.

What Randy was aggressively trying to point out was the fact that Hypercom had sued these two men by accusing them of doing things they had never intended to do. *"Had you told anyone at Hypercom that you were leaving to go to Ingenico because of a conspiracy between you and Mr. Boardman and Ms. Shipley to steal trade—to misappropriate trade secrets and confidential information?"* Randy once again asked.

With the defense once again objecting and the court once again overruling, Bernie answered, *"Emphatically, absolutely not!"*

Randy continued to ask questions to bring to light that many Hypercom employees in the past had left the company but none was sued, let alone accused of stealing trade secrets. Throughout his questioning the defense continued to object and in most instances the court continued to overrule. Finally Randy asked, *"What was the ultimate result of the lawsuit that was filed against you?"*

"Hypercom voluntarily dismissed the lawsuit," Bernie explained.

With that you could see the surprised looks on the faces of the jurors—

almost a look of "you've got to be kidding." I think it became clear to many members of the jury at that moment that Hypercom had simply filed these lawsuits out of pure retaliation to my having sued them.

Randy didn't stop there though. He went on to inquire of Bernie whether he knew that when Hypercom sued him and Greg that they had also sued me personally. Again the defense tried to overrule any discussion of this, but again the court overruled.

Bernie responded that he was unaware because during that time neither Bernie nor Greg nor I was allowed to have any communication between one another.

"After the suit was dropped were you able, then, to finally have a conversation with Lisa?" Randy asked.

"Yes, yes," Bernie confirmed.

"When you were able to finally have those conversations with Lisa were you able to make observations as to how those lawsuits and the allegations that Hypercom had made had impacted her?"

Bernie choked up as he responded. *"Yeah. She was—words are tough on this one. She was upset and emotionally disturbed by the fact that this had happened. She was distraught; there's the word.*

"I don't think that instantly overnight the sun came out and everything was fine. It takes a while to get over that kind of stuff, you know. I also had those feelings, so I have an idea of the timelines, and, you know, what I saw was that it lingered."

With that, Randy's direct ended and the court took a half-hour break before Charlie began his cross-examination.

|||||||||

Early into his cross-examination Charlie addressed the issue of Bernie waiting for his commission before resigning from Hypercom. His questioning became very accusatory, with question after question trying to make it sound like there had been some conspiracy between Bernie and Greg to resign at the same time.

"Isn't it true that when you spoke to the assistant general counsel of Hypercom that it was Ingenico that requested that you and Mr. Boardman resign on the same day?"

Fed up with the almost badgering line of questioning, Bernie had apparently had as much as he could tolerate. He pounded his fist on the witness stand, leaned forward, and vehemently denied the accusation.

"That is absolutely not true," he insisted. *"I never said that to anyone, ever. I said the opposite of that, and it is absolutely not true."* The indignation shown by Bernie demonstrated just how much he was offended by being accused of not telling the truth.

Charlie quickly switched the subject, moving to questions about a comment Bernie had made earlier regarding the "challenging culture."

"And by that you meant that there were going to be stricter requirements posed in order to make more money, correct?" Charlie asked, trying to establish that Philippe was merely making changes that would tighten things up, changes that the salespeople would naturally not like.

"Well, when I referred to the challenging culture it was a more broad statement, but part of the challenging culture was the compensation plans, yes," Bernie clarified.

Charlie tried to suggest that Hypercom didn't treat woman differently but actually elevated them when he asked Bernie about the woman who had been hired to replace me.

"In fact she was not only given Ms. Shipley's job, but she was given a bigger job, that is, she was made managing director for the Americas, correct?"

"Yes," Bernie simply acknowledged.

Appearing to accentuate the point, he added, *"And that included not only North America, which Ms. Shipley had, but also South America and Central America as well, correct?"*

Again, rather passively, Bernie simply responded, *"Yes."*

Charlie had done his best to make his point. With that, cross-examination ended and Bernie was dismissed.

Next up on the witness stand would be Greg Boardman. My lawyers saw Greg as my biggest risk going into the trial. Greg had actually taken some documents from Hypercom when he left, although it was later proven in Hypercom's case against him that the documents he took were not confidential. Still, we worried whether his credibility would hold up with the jury. But Greg had definitely seen Philippe's treatment toward me, and ultimately we felt he could do more to help us than to harm. We would soon see if we were right or wrong.

- 11 -

CASUALTIES
OF THE BATTLE

As Greg took the stand I was reminded of how much all the stress
had changed him. He was no longer the strong, gregarious Greg
I once knew. His once confident demeanor had diminished; he seemed
extremely reserved and humble. The lawsuit Hypercom filed against Greg
and all the repercussions from it had absolutely broken him—financially
and spiritually. During this time of despair he had strengthened his
religious belief and he wore a large cross that hung from a chain around
his neck to demonstrate his strong faith.

David handled the direct examination. He began by taking Greg
through his 11 years at Hypercom in relation to his knowing and working
with me, right up to when Philippe came on board.

"*Was Philippe Tartavull confrontational with everybody?*" David asked.

"*Philippe was generally a confrontational person,*" Greg explained. "*But
with respect to the managing directors I felt like he amped it up another notch
for Lisa.*"

Moving on to the subject of the Cartes trade show, David asked if
Greg thought it was unusual that I had not attended.

"I did feel like that was unusual, yes," he said. *"When you have a trade show, certainly a global trade show, I think Philippe's position was, well, this isn't a U.S. show. That was kind of the position. Couldn't be further from the truth. We've got a number of customers in the industry. In fact the biggest ones, First Data, whom Lisa had a tight relationship with, Global Payments, Elavon, these are global customers. There's global pricing strategies that are put in place and if you are not there to represent your region, then the folks who attend those shows from your region, customers of yours, will inevitably get an undivided audience with your competition."* His testimony, like Bernie's, made it quite clear why my attendance at the show would have been appropriate and valuable.

Since Hypercom had sued Greg personally for going to work at Ingenico and supposedly conspiring with me to steal proprietary information, David delved into that period of time, asking Greg about his departure from the company.

Greg took a long time to explain that early on he had had some conversations with the president of Ingenico and had discussed going to work for them. *"I liked the idea,"* Greg admitted. *"Things had progressively gotten worse at Hypercom; felt like I was starting to move into a position of exclusion, which is kind of the zone of treatment from Philippe Tartavull that signals the beginning of the end if you're used to working for him. So the prospect of going to Ingenico was relatively appealing. Lisa worked there. Of course I had a very good working relationship with her. I learned shortly thereafter that Bernie Frey, a good friend of mine who was the head of the sales organization at Hypercom, had also had conversations with Ingenico. And the prospect of us all working together again really appealed to me."*

Greg went on to explain that two weeks before giving his formal resignation he had advised Philippe's chief of staff and three other managers that he was going to be leaving Hypercom. He had also told his boss that he was leaving, even notifying her where he was going. *"So they knew where I was going and I obliged in training my successors, moving data from my hard drive, from my email to assist them in getting transitioned and taking over my duties. The rest of that week is a bit of a blur, but more like a nightmare,"* Greg said.

David asked Greg to explain why it was a nightmare. He explained that he had quit on a Monday and started training his successors shortly thereafter but was advised on Wednesday that he would not be needed beyond that day.

"I said, okay, fine, I still have a few other folks to train. She [Greg's boss] *said okay, fine. They sent one of the IT personnel to my home to pick up my laptop on Thursday, hand over any other property that I had that belonged to Hypercom. I obliged, gave them the media. On Friday I went out to relax because I figured I have some down time now—they don't need me. I'm going to take the opportunity to relax.*

"I came home to a very frantic wife. My wife also worked at Hypercom at the exact time that this was going on and remained employed at Hypercom until earlier this year. But she was frantic and said we've been served and it's Hypercom.

"I didn't believe her at first. I said, you're kidding me. I couldn't fathom what was going on. It just didn't make any sense to me. I opened a packet, which was their complaint, their lodged complaint. And I got maybe four pages into it and I called Chris Justice [the president of Ingenico] *in a panic. I felt entrapped. I thought I had nowhere to go and it looked like I was in serious trouble. To say that I was stunned and shocked would be an understatement."*

You could see the pained look on his face and the weariness in his eyes as he was challenged to relive what to him had been a huge nightmare.

David continued, referring to an exhibit that dealt with a ruling from Greg's case.

"In the first paragraph, I'm going to read it to you, the third sentence from the judge's order, it says, 'This industry is very dynamic with top-level employees regularly switching employment with top-level competitors without restriction or consequence to the former employer.' Was that true from your experience

leading up to the time this lawsuit was filed?" David asked.

"It remains true," Greg replied. *"Hypercom has since hired a number of individuals from Ingenico in fact."*

David then referred to another paragraph, saying, *"There's a sentence that says, 'The court finds the plaintiff failed to establish that Mr. Boardman actually has disclosed confidential information to Ingenico either verbally or in writing.' Was that true at the time?"*

"It was true," Greg replied.

"And you had testified that you had no desire to harm Hypercom and disclose confidential information in the hearing?" David asked.

"I did," Greg responded. *"As I stated, my wife worked there. I had a number of close friendships. I was a stockholder. To think that I had any notion of harming Hypercom was ridiculous."*

When David tried to enter one more exhibit pertaining to the lawsuit against Greg, the defense objected, claiming this lawsuit had nothing to do with Greg. But the court overruled and David moved on. It wasn't long before the defense objected again, which led to a somewhat lengthy back-and-forth debate between the defense, David, and the court. Finally the court clarified exactly what could and could not be discussed and David proceeded through more of Hypercom's claims, asking Greg to read them and following up with questions regarding the authenticity of each.

"What does paragraph 111 say?" David asked. This was an example of the kind of questions he continued to ask Greg.

Greg read from the document: *"Mr. Boardman, Ms. Shipley and Ingenico conspired to and did misappropriate trade secrets and confidential and/or proprietary information belonging to Hypercom for the benefit of defendants."*

"Did you engage in any conspiracy with Ms. Shipley to misappropriate trade secrets or confidential information?" David asked.

"Absolutely not," Greg answered.

"Did you tell anyone at Hypercom that you were conspiring with Ms.

Shipley to steal trade secrets or misappropriate confidential information?"

"No, I did not," replied Greg.

David wanted to show the jury just how callous Hypercom had been with the accusations. His final questioning vividly revealed how scheming Hypercom had been.

Referring to one last exhibit, David asked Greg to explain the document.

"It is a confidentiality settlement agreement and mutual release," Greg explained—the agreement that resolved Hypercom's suit against Greg.

But when David made a motion to admit the exhibit the defense objected, saying, *"I'm not sure what the relevance is of this—his settlement, with the settlement document in his case to this case."* Apparently, they did not want this information discussed.

But the court overruled, and David moved on and asked about a paragraph that referenced an interview. *"Tell me what you recall and what you know about that,"* he asked of Greg.

"As a part of the agreement to settle with Hypercom in my case they wanted me to have an interview with their attorneys and discuss details surrounding my hiring at Ingenico and things that pertain to what I believe was my case," Greg explained.

"You thought it was going to be about your case when you agreed to it?" David asked.

"I did."

"So what was the tone of the questioning?" David inquired.

"The questions about my case seemed really perfunctory, like they weren't very serious about it. I was asked a great deal of questions about Lisa Shipley though."

"If you recall, what were some of these questions that they asked you about Lisa?" David asked.

"I think they asked me if I had ever witnessed Philippe discriminate against Lisa. Did she ever ask me for confidential information, or, you know, in the course of my job did I give any information to her, questions like that."

Greg confirmed that his answer had been "no," that Lisa had never asked him about confidential information.

David then read from the document, asking Greg if he understood what the sentence was directed at. The sentence read:

"*Hypercom expressly agrees that the preceding sentence is not intended to and will not in any way limit Hypercom's use of the information provided by Boardman, whether in the interview or affidavit, in any proceeding or lawsuit to which Boardman is not a party.*"

Greg admitted that he was not clear about the intent. So David, through additional questions, made it clear that at the time of Greg being interviewed, my lawsuit was still active. He inferred that the interview with Greg was most likely directed to gain information that Hypercom might be able to use against me in my lawsuit against them.

Believing that he had made his point, David concluded his direct examination.

| | | | | | | | | | |

Charlie began cross-examination by asking Greg to confirm that Hypercom had paid for him to receive an Executive MBA degree and implied that in relation to that he had signed an agreement—an agreement that he would later realize was a confidentiality and non-compete agreement. But Greg was quick to point out that the two were not connected.

"*That* [the agreement] *was not in conjunction or in exchange for that benefit; no,*" Greg emphasized.

Ignoring the clarification and emphasizing the point that Greg had signed an agreement, Charlie went on.

"*You did sign that agreement did you not?*"

"*I did sign the agreement, but not in conjunction with the MBA,*" Greg pointed out again. His answer seemed to irritate Charlie.

"*This will go faster if you stick to my question,*" he sarcastically snapped back. *"I simply asked whether you signed the agreement. And, I gather the answer was yes."*

Charlie went on to state that in that agreement Greg had promised not to disclose Hypercom's confidential information to anyone and promised not to go directly from Hypercom to work for a competitor.

"After reading the document, once it was put in front of me again for review during the trial, I became aware of the stipulations of the non-compete portion," Greg explained. *"At the time that I signed it, it was in a hurried fashion. I did not review the document,"* he confessed. *"But, yes, that's my signature on it."*

Hitting hard on Greg's failure to adhere to the agreement, Charlie went on to point out that the agreement forbid him from going to work for a competitor and that Ingenico was specifically named in the agreement as a competitor.

"But, that's exactly what you did, didn't you? You resigned from Hypercom and you attempted to go to work directly for Ingenico, correct?" Charlie sternly asked.

"I did," Greg admitted.

Then trying his best to bring me into Greg's decision to leave Hypercom he said, *"And in fact it is true that in the summer of 2009 Ms. Shipley recruited you to come to work at Ingenico, correct?"*

"That is not true," Greg adamantly responded. *"Chris Justice recruited me to work for Ingenico."*

Ignoring the correction Charlie moved his line of questioning to the issue of stolen documents.

"Now, isn't it true, Mr. Boardman, that you stole thousands of confidential Hypercom documents on your way out the door?"

Obviously offended, Greg flared back. *"I did not steal documents from Hypercom. No! I did a backup of my computer. I had backups, older backups from previous backups that I had done, by the way, which were encouraged by our IT department. And I had that information, but I did not deprive them of the information. That was not deleted. And in fact I organized much of it and returned it back to my successors that I trained."*

Charlie didn't give up though, suggesting that there was confidential information on his personal computer and his laptop, to which Greg had to agree that there might have been. With that Charlie proceeded as if he were closing in on a guilty man.

"Now, Hypercom sued you because you violated your agreement and you stole those documents that we've just been talking about, correct?"

Once again, offended by what seemed to be twisting the truth of the situation, Greg responded. *"I was sued for the non-compete agreement, and—I was alleged to have taken information for the purposes of providing it to Ingenico, but again, the phrase 'stealing,' I don't agree with the phrasing."*

Charlie continued on this vein, identifying every little detail that he felt could possibly make Greg come across as dishonest and unreliable. By the expression on some of the jurors' faces I wondered if the jury was buying it all—to me at least they were beginning to have some real empathy for Greg being treated so harshly.

When Charlie apparently felt like he had beaten the topic to death he moved on. His next question seemed tentative, however; at minimum it was phrased in a very disjointed manner.

"Now, after about four months on the job, you got hired, you got hired, you left Hypercom in August of 2009. And, but in early January of 2010 Ingenico fired you, correct?"

Despite the awkward phrasing of the question, Greg confirmed that this was correct.

"And the reason why you were fired was because you stole those Hypercom documents, isn't that right?" Charlie hammered.

"I was never given the reason for my termination, but I believed that it was associated with the fact that I had produced that information later," Greg responded.

Charlie dragged out the humiliating information with more questions about his being fired and finally asked, *"You weren't even surprised when you got fired, were you?"*

"I was not," Greg admitted.

With few additional questions Charlie ended his cross-examination. It was painful to watch, but David quickly asked to redirect; he felt he needed to clarify some of Greg's answers.

"Whatever happened with all that electronic information? Do you know?" David asked.

"Well interesting, I produced it," Greg said. *"The Hypercom attorneys, I believe, did forensics analysis on it to look for anything that was confidential or anything that I may have used in conjunction with my employment at Ingenico. And when they finished with that they gave me all the electronic media back with every piece of information still populated on it."*

Even though Greg had never been given an actual reason for being fired from Ingenico, at least he got the opportunity to let the jury know that despite accusations of stealing confidential information, nothing on his computer had been found to be confidential.

Shortly thereafter Greg was excused and the court recessed for lunch.

It was emotional for me to sit back while Bernie and Greg testified. I had that motherly feeling of wanting to help them, when of course I knew I couldn't. It's such a hopeless feeling to watch someone you care about deeply be on the witness stand and be torn apart by one of New York's finest attorneys.

It had been a long, emotional morning and we were all ready for a break.

| | | | | | | | | | |

The first witness following lunch was Ed Labry, president of First Data, the company that had been my largest customer and the man who was now my current boss. Ed looks like your ideal corporate president. He has a very inviting smile and an overall, down-to-earth personal manner that conveys warmth and caring. He easily engages and draws you to him. You could see by the surprised expression on many of the jurors' faces when he confirmed that the company was in the $11 billion range that they were impressed he was voluntarily testifying on my behalf.

Ed explained that he had known me for 15 to 20 years, having first met me when he was with a company that transitioned from manufacturing electronic processing equipment to the processing side of the business. At that time the company had made a decision to buy their equipment from VeriFone. But, as he explained, I didn't let that keep me from trying to get some of their business.

"I got approached probably monthly for a couple of years by this lady named Lisa Shipley that was trying to get us to use Hypercom terminals rather than VeriFone terminals," he explained.

David asked if there came a time that they started using Hypercom terminals and Ed responded, *"Yes."*

When asked to elaborate on the decision, Ed explained that while you could have five or six different terminals, all would be recognizable as credit card processing machines. *"But what you don't know, they're made by different companies. But they're all made of plastic and they're all made of parts that probably come from Taiwan and you really can't tell them apart.*

"I think the thing that separates the companies in the processing industry are, number one, the functionality of the terminal, but two, really the individual that's representing the company to us.

"One of the things that Lisa brought to the table was not just selling to an Ed Labry or selling to our procurement, she had actually worked with the company all the way through the sales force, even down to the salesman level, and created incentive programs and so forth to help our company sell their product that differentiated from the four or five different terminals that we stocked in our warehouses."

David inquired as to the amount of business that First Data did with Hypercom.

"If I had to say one number it was $20 to $25 million a year in terminals."

"And, who was the salesperson in '07 for Hypercom that sold these terminals to First Data?" David asked.

"Lisa Shipley," Ed responded.

You may remember that one of my claims in filing this lawsuit had been that Philippe never visited any of my clients—particularly First Data—despite the huge amount of business they did with us. David's next question confirmed my allegation.

"Did Mr. Tartavull ever come to see you on a sales call with Ms. Shipley in 2007?" he asked.

"No, I don't believe so," Ed responded.

"Did you find it unusual that Mr. Tartavull never came on a sales call with Ms. Shipley to First Data in 2007?" David continued.

"I would say that I find it unusual just because historically I had great relationships with other CEOs of VeriFone and actually former CEOs of Hypercom. Yes," Ed explained.

David then asked if other Hypercom CEOs had visited him, with me, and named specific CEOs prior to Philippe. One by one Ed responded "yes."

"Do you believe it was helpful for the Hypercom CEO to visit with you?" David asked.

"Yes. I like to have a relationship with the peer or the peer element at the company you're doing business with just in case there are problems."

Next, David had Ed confirm that I now worked for First Data and that he had been aware of the lawsuit I had filed as well as the lawsuit that Hypercom had filed against me personally. David asked him how he thought the lawsuits impacted me.

"I think when you are in a small boutique industry and you build your career, being sued with certain allegations, you carry those around and it weighs on you, especially this is where you make your livelihood and there's only four or five companies that are in the industry—that are in the terminal industry. So I think she was pretty devastated by it."

Ed was very forthcoming and sincere, and I felt that his testimony had been well received by the jury. David thanked Ed and ended his examination. Evidently, the defense realized that anything they asked of

Ed would do little to benefit their position so they chose not to cross-examine him.

|||||||||||

Next to take the stand was Chris Justice, president of Ingenico and my former boss. As I said previously, Justice is the perfect name for Chris. To me, he was Superman; he supported all of us during the unprecedented lawsuits filed against Bernie, Greg, and me personally. At 6 foot 4 Chris has a presence when he walks into a room. He dresses immaculately, right down to his highly polished shoes. He is well spoken with a charming, slow, deliberate southern drawl. I knew he would be an impressive witness for us, particularly because when Hypercom filed their lawsuit against me they chose not to include Ingenico, even though it was the company I had supposedly supplied stolen information to. Chris insisted they include Ingenico in Hypercom's suit against me so he could adequately defend me. It was so symbolic of his high standard of ethics and his determination to do what he believed was right.

David Ritter continued to handle the direct examination, and after confirming Chris's position at Ingenico David went immediately to the topic of the lawsuits filed by Hypercom.

"When you were at Ingenico did Hypercom sue Ingenico?" he asked.

"Yes sir," Chris replied.

"Do you recall who Hypercom sued?"

"They filed three simultaneous lawsuits against Bernie Frey, Greg Boardman, and Lisa Shipley personally," Chris said.

"Even though Hypercom did not sue Ingenico along with Ms. Shipley, did Ingenico become involved in that case?" David probed.

"Yes sir," Chris confirmed.

"Why?"

"Because I wasn't going to allow an industry competitor to bully my employees," Chris stated firmly.

David went on to confirm that Ingenico hired lawyers to defend the company and all three employees. But when he inquired as to how much Ingenico paid its lawyers to defend all three, the defense objected, stating that the issue was irrelevant. This caused considerable back-and-forth discussion between the lawyers and the court. Finally the court said, *"Well she's [Lisa] implicated in those lawsuits though. Particularly in the Boardman suit that was testified earlier, the allegations against Ingenico in that suit have to be against Ms. Shipley because she's the only Ingenico employee at that time. So I think that is sort of relevant in that respect.*

"I do think he can testify about those expenses to give it some perspective for the jurors. So I'll overrule the objection."

With that Chris was allowed to confirm that the total cost was a whopping $400,000 to $500,000.

"Do you recall what these lawsuits were about that you were involved in?" David asked.

"Well, basically the Frey and Boardman cases or the assumption on Hypercom's part is that we were hiring both employees to steal trade secrets. Ingenico was not pulled into the Shipley aspect of it, but, as I recall, the suit filed against her was for conspiracy," Chris explained.

"Conspiracy to do what?" David challenged.

With that the defense again objected, stating that the court documents spoke for themselves and it wasn't necessary for the witness to give his recollection. But the court disagreed and overruled the objection.

"What were the allegations in the Shipley case?" David continued.

"They were alleging it was a conspiracy. I think to steal trade secrets or to steal employees. It was a little bit vague," explained Chris.

Chris was then asked about the hiring of both Bernie and Greg.

"In your years of experience in the industry is it unusual for employees to move back and forth between competitors such as Hypercom, VeriFone, and Ingenico?" David asked.

"Players change jerseys and play for different teams all the time," Chris confirmed, adding, *"Well, in fact, Philippe Tartavull was personally involved in hiring two of the top retail people from Ingenico even after he had filed a lawsuit against us for taking employees from Hypercom."*

Chris then responded that in his recollection no one had sued anyone for anything close to Hypercom's suit. He also stated that customers are no secret either. *"You can look right there on the counter and see who's doing business with whom,"* pointing out that the vendor's name is right on the equipment.

"Let me ask you about the technology for these credit card processing machines," David said. *"Was that secret when you were president of Ingenico?"*

Chris responded that it was not, saying, *"The feature functionality is all clearly listed on everybody's website."* These two areas alone made the whole issue of secrecy seem rather ridiculous.

David then moved to questions about Chris having a discussion with Hypercom's chief of staff about settling the lawsuits. He asked what was said in that conversation.

"That conversation Clint [Jones, Hypercom's chief of staff] *basically had told me that they had made several assumptions as to why they thought Ingenico was trying to steal trade secrets and they thought that those assumptions were proven wrong in Arizona, and therefore, they just wanted to back out and let us, Ingenico, walk away; all the while, though, they were going to continue to carry on their lawsuit against Boardman, Frey, and Shipley individually,"* Chris explained.

"What was your response to that offer?"

"I turned it down categorically. They weren't going to come in and continue to try to bully my employees and chase away good people."

David turned his questioning to how Chris thought all the lawsuits impacted me.

"I think they impacted her quite a bit," Chris said. *"They certainly impacted everybody from the standpoint that it's an intense time drain to basically have*

lawsuits launched, your reputation thrown under the bus, just about every other aspect of it is very time consuming. I think for Lisa individually it's a very personal thing for her to have her reputation drug through the mud, to be called a thief, to be called a scoundrel and all the things that were basically alleged."

"Did she ever become emotional in dealing with these issues? Did she cry?" David asked.

"Oh certainly, certainly. Tearing up, yes. I guess I kind of would categorize crying more as just boohooing or sobbing. But tearing up, definitely," Chris said.

When asked why he had directed me not to speak with certain other employees at Ingenico—specifically Bernie and Greg—Chris said, *"Because of all the allegations that there was this conspiracy and that there was all of this stuff going on. So we spent time with our legal counsel who said the best course of action until we gain clarity on how these cases are going to play out is to not allow the three of them to be actively involved together with the company."*

Finally, David questioned Chris on the fact that he had terminated Greg. *"Why did you terminate him?"* David asked.

"Through all of the discovery process we had continued to say that, first of all, there are no trade secrets in our industry, but beyond that we didn't want any confidential information. It was forbidden to be brought into the company. And Hypercom kept alleging that there were other devices and other things that were out there that Greg had in his possession of which Greg was telling me that he had none of that. So to satisfy our own needs, to make sure we were clean, we, Ingenico, collected his computer, had it scrubbed, and it was found that a USB drive that had a Hypercom label, some kind of electronic tag or something, had been inserted into the device. And so because he had gone against what I had told him, which is 'don't bring anything of theirs here to the company,' even though I don't think anything was actually used, it was still plugged in and therefore we terminated him."

David then asked him who Greg was currently working for. *"Ingenico,"* Chris said, admitting that he, Chris Justice, had hired Greg back about a year after terminating him.

"Why did you hire him back?" David asked.

"Because he's really good at what he does. He's a darn good employee."

"And were you concerned about him taking Hypercom information?" David questioned.

"First of all, we had already settled all of the other lawsuits. Secondly, they had given him back all of the devices that they had taken from him—they gave all the information back, which again proved to me that there were no trade secrets here to be stolen. And third, told him that, hey, everybody's allowed to make a bad call every now and then, but I don't want to see it again going forward. So he agreed to be much more candid and up front and hired him back."

That ended David's examination. The defendant's cross-examination basically went nowhere and ended rather quickly.

We all believed that Chris had been a great witness for me, particularly by providing reality for the jury of just how spiteful Hypercom's suits against all of us had been, and by making it pretty clear that Hypercom's suit against me was pure retaliation.

It felt like the day should be ended, but half the afternoon was still left. That meant when we returned from lunch, I would be testifying. Although I was apprehensive I was also excited.

Finally, I was going to be able to tell the jury my story.

- 12 -

MY TURN TO TESTIFY

As I stepped to the witness stand I took a deep breath to calm my nerves. The time had finally come for me to tell my story. I so wanted the jury to like me, but more important, I wanted them to see me as credible. My greatest concern was the discussion that would transpire about my commission plan and my not making as much as my male peers. I knew that by most people's standards I made a lot of money, and I didn't want to sound unappreciative. I wanted the jury to understand that my fight was about fairness, and I wanted them to see beyond the numbers. I just had to remember to slow down and think about my answers before responding. I trusted that Randy, through his questions, would steer me in the right direction.

Randy began by asking me to put into my own words what caused me to be here in the midst of this trial.

"After an amazing 11 years at a company that I loved and a job that I loved, Philippe Tartavull came into Hypercom on my 12th year there and everything changed. I was treated very differently than my male counterparts. I came to find out that I was compensated differently than my

male counterparts. I fought to make things right and when I couldn't and I left, a frivolous lawsuit was filed against me at my new employer and it's caused me a lot of harm to this day."

Randy next wanted the jury to hear about my career journey and how I had worked hard to become the highest-ranking woman at Hypercom. He wanted them to know that I had earned it. He started back at my college days and had me explain how as one of nine children I had to work my way through college and how I got my first job in banking, which eventually led me into the electronic credit card equipment industry. He asked me about awards I had won and about all my previous bosses and how each one had acknowledged and valued my work ethic. It all seemed to go quite smoothly until he began to ask about commissions that I received in 2005, two years before Philippe came on the scene. The defense immediately objected and continued to object regardless of how Randy rephrased his questions. It finally culminated in a bench conference where both lawyers argued back and forth the relevance of my commission structure at a time when my role was not yet managing director.

Obviously this was going to be a contentious topic. Even when it appeared that the court had made it clear what could be asked, the defense immediately objected when Randy asked, *"Ms. Shipley, in the year prior to 2007, do you recall what your earnings were?"* Once again the lawyers argued back and forth until the court stated, *"At this time I'm going to stand by the ruling. I'm going to take it under consideration, but for right now you can explore her compensation plan and the differences in the plan and any income she may have earned in '06 and realized in '07. I'm going to give it further thought and may allow you to go back, but right now let's move on."*

Randy was finally free to ask me how my compensation plan was set in 2006. I responded with a lot of detail, hoping the jury would understand not only the complexity of the commission plan but also how important it was to my overall earnings. I realized that I was quite shaky when I started my testimony, not always being succinct and clear. It took me a little time to settle in, but in time it became easier. From here Randy asked about what happened early in 2007.

"Early on in 2007 I was approached by O.B. and asked to consider taking the managing director position within North America.

"It was a very prestigious position in our company—that title is well-known across players in the industry. So it was enticing to me. I clearly saw that as a promotion. It included what I was told would be additional compensation both in base and variable comp."

"Were you told that your job would be different from what the other managing directors were doing?" Randy asked.

"Absolutely not," I responded.

"Help us understand at a corporate level how high up is this position in the company?"

I explained, *"It's as high up as you can go—I mean the next step would be Philippe Tartavull's position."*

"And did you engage directly with the president of the company or the CEO? Was that the managing director's job to engage with them on strategic decisions," Randy asked.

"Sure. I would be part of the executive management team and have regular dialogues about the strategy for the company. I was considered an insider so I couldn't sell stock, for instance, at certain times of the year because of the knowledge that I received. I was the highest ranking female in the company."

"Let's talk a little bit about the experiences in that time with the managing director position," Randy said. *"What were you told about your compensation when you took the job?"*

"I had a lot of discussion with O.B. about whether to take this position—a lot. I didn't want to get boxed into a position that was not as or more lucrative than what I was used to making.

"I had a lot of dialogue about making sure that this package was indeed a promotion and not just a title, but in compensation. And I was told that it would be and that I was asked to trust him, that they weren't ready yet to put

a plan in front of me, but that the company would do the right thing, and I believed him."

Randy asked if I had any knowledge of how managing directors had been compensated previously.

"In talking to O.B., I was clearly told that the plans would be fair and equal to the other managing directors. The only variable that stuck out was a slight difference in the way that they would pay the managing directors, based on the size of the region and the revenue that these managing directors were producing," I explained.

"And were the plans as far as you understood structured in the same way with this base pay and incentive compensation?" Randy tried to clarify.

"I was told they were."

Randy then asked about the time period that Philippe came on board. I explained that he came on board as interim president in February. *"We were told that there was a CEO search on and that he would be filling that role until the CEO position could be filled."*

Randy returned to compensation plan issues. *"Did it get put into place?"* he asked.

"It was a battle," I exclaimed. *"You have to understand prior to 2007 I was paid monthly on not just my base pay, but on my commissions. I got a monthly commission check. I was very used to that. I understood as a managing director that the way I would be paid and the timing that I would be paid would be different. It would be based like the other managing directors, which would be quarterly. I was okay with that.*

"First of all I was offered a $50,000 base increase as part of this plan—just trust us, this comp plan will come. So I waited. I waited to receive the base pay increase. I waited to get a comp plan. I regularly, weekly, monthly, complained to O.B. that I wanted a plan. I didn't know what my targets were. I took the job in good faith and I didn't know how I was going to be paid."

I explained that soon it was April and I still didn't have a plan. When I asked O.B. about it he told me that it was in Philippe's hands to approve.

Randy then asked me about an email that I received from Philippe in which he told me that he was going to get my compensation plan done and apologized. He wrote that it was on top of his list to get done. I explained that he never followed through.

Randy then showed me another email—one I had written to O.B. pleading to get the base salary I had been promised and for my plan to be finalized. It was now the end of May and I had been waiting since February and still had not received any commissions.

Randy presented another email following a conversation I had had with Philippe asking him what had happened to my commission plan. In Philippe's response he said that it had to be approved by something called the compensation committee. I'd never heard of that group before and didn't know what it was, so I questioned it. I looked up the group to see what authority it had and questioned whether Philippe needed to go to the compensation committee to sign off on my comp plan.

"Did the compensation committee have to sign off on your comp plan?" Randy asked.

"Not that I'm aware of, no."

"Did he follow up on this with you?" Randy asked.

"No."

"So," said Randy, *"my understanding, then, is that he had told you the reason for the delay was something that you learned to be untrue."*

"That's correct," I confirmed.

Randy asked, *"But you didn't receive the compensation that was promised to you, at least the base salary, until June."*

"That's correct."

"How did you feel during this time period when you were doing this work with a raise that had been promised to you but not been delivered?" Randy asked.

"I felt like I had a bit of a bait and switch. I trusted that the company was going to do what they said they would do and I felt cheated and disrespected."

"What was the explanation that was given to you?" Randy asked.

"I was told it was held up by Philippe."

I explained that even after a plan was finally approved I was never paid according to that plan. *"I fought every commission payment that was made to me in 2007. It was a quarterly event. Things got held up by Philippe. I don't believe I was ever paid on time relative to what should have been paid. You close a quarter at the end of June you should get a July commission check. If you close the quarter at the end of September you should get an October commission. And not only were they not paid timely, there was a fight about what the amount should be."*

|| | | | | | | | | |

"Let me step back from compensation only for a minute and ask you a little bit just to describe what the first few months at the beginning of what it was like working with Philippe Tartavull," Randy said.

"Not like anything I had ever experienced in 25 years in this business," I said. *"I'd worked for every kind of business that you can imagine—in fact, all men. I'd never worked for a woman in 20 years, except maybe in the very early days of Sovereign Bank. I had reported to men my entire career. I was revered in the company. I'm trying to think of the right word to say. The company loved me and I loved them and people fought to be recognized and to be at the same level of recognition with the company. And so when Philippe came in, I certainly wanted to like him like I liked all the other bosses. I certainly wanted him to like me back.*

"There was an immediate attitude with Philippe that I had perceived, an immediate lack of respect for who I am, what I represented to the company that I worked for. He was increasingly dismissive. My opinions didn't matter. I didn't have support, the day-to-day support that you would expect from any manager. You would expect regular meetings. You would expect phone calls. You would expect a career plan and dialogue with your boss of how you're going to achieve and be successful in the role that you're in. There was complete and utter not only disrespect but alienation. I was put on an island and just ignored."

Randy then had me look at an email that Philippe had sent to me after I had been on the job just seven days. Philippe had copied all my peers. In my opinion, he was attacking what was happening in the North American market and why the numbers were not where they needed to be.

"We had no prior dialogue, no sit-down about the climate, the environment, what's happening in the industry, what's happening with customers. This was just, in my opinion, kind of a first attack before even having any dialogue on the subject whatsoever. And the fact that he copied my peers on the email, I thought it was very disrespectful."

"So when you talked to O.B. about this public form of humiliation, is that because he was copying your peers on an email that you didn't think needed to be published?" Randy asked.

"Yeah, I think some of this between an employee and a boss is one-on-one dialogue. I mean, if you're going to give criticism, there's ways professionally to do that, especially at this level in the company. Absolutely."

"Okay. But to be fair, did you see similar types of criticism of the European market from Philippe on emails like this? Would he send emails like this criticizing EMA or Asia-Pacific or South America?"

"No, never. I never saw him reprimand the other MDs [managing directors] *in writing."*

To further indicate Philippe's lack of communicating with me, Randy asked, *"Did he have a habit of saying let's talk more about something when you would raise a concern with him?"*

I explained, *"Philippe only communicated with me in email, period. We did not have weekly calls. In fact in the history of ten months working for the man we never had a one-on-one meeting. I never had a meeting with my boss.*

"Literally there was no attempt ever to sit down, talk with me, to pick up the phone and talk to me. His preference in communicating with me was strictly email."

Randy then asked, *"What would happen when he would say, let's talk more?"*

"Nothing," I said. *"There are times when he would say, 'Set up a time or send me a request,' and I had to go through his assistant, which I did, and nothing would happen after that."*

Some of the most humiliating times for me were the managing director meetings, where all of us had to follow the same format and report on revenues, margins, and what our forecasting looked like. So Randy asked me to talk about those meetings and how I felt Philippe treated me in those meetings.

"I think the number one word that comes to mind is just complete disrespect. I knew the U.S. market better than anyone in the company. He didn't want to hear my opinions about the landscape, the customers. He was on the attack. When I would get up, it would be just a series of one question after another where it was just—it felt like being attacked. I was always to go first in these meetings, which had its own ramifications in itself."

"Why did it matter that you went first?" Randy asked.

"I was the sacrificial lamb for the other managing directors. These meetings were tough. And Philippe was tough. But to have to go first and to hear all the questions that the CEO of the company's drilling at you, having somebody go first allows you to sit back, know the questions that he's going to ask you, and have time to prepare so that when he asks you those similar questions, that you're ready.

"He was critical of my suggestions in making changes and how we could grow the business. There was no pleasing him. The meetings were brutal."

"How did you react to the way he treated you in these meetings," Randy asked.

"Just defeated, just defeated. I couldn't make him happy. I couldn't give him what he wanted. My peers saw it. There was empathy. Everyone recognized the way that he treated me. Not everyone will admit they recognized it, but I had a lot of consoling from peers that I have a lot of respect from that said, 'What's going on? Why the attack and why is he treating you like this?'

"He gave me the title, but he never gave me the authority or the respect of the role."

"*Did you get the sense that one of the reasons why you were being treated like this was because you were a woman?*" Randy asked.

"*Absolutely I did.*"

"*Why?*"

"*Because he didn't treat any of the men the same way. Because my compensation was not the same, because benefits that my peers had and that I asked for were not given.*"

Randy later referred to an email that I had sent to Philippe, again expressing my concern that my commission payments were delayed and that I couldn't understand why.

I said, "*I'm venting here that I'm now in this position for almost eight months and that I've taken a serious cut in pay from where I was prior to coming into this role.*

"*I felt like maybe some of the hostility coming my way, that maybe there was something I could address there with him and certainly said that if he had questions I was more than willing to talk to him about that.*"

Randy asked, "*How about this next to the last paragraph? 'Philippe I do not feel as though I've had your support since you've come on board.' What led you to write that?*"

I responded, "*Just the fact that the only way that he'd communicate to me was in email and it was always questioning my performance, the region, what it was doing, no strategizing about how to be successful in this role. It was always more of a tactic with him, if you will. But clearly I was very frustrated, saying I don't understand it. I'm trying to get your support. I'm trying to do what you want me to do, but that, no, I never felt like I had his support from the time he walked in the door and I made it clear in this email.*"

We next covered the fact that O.B. had been told he would be leaving the company as early as May and I would be reporting directly to Philippe.

"*Are you attempting to work out a better work relationship?*" Randy asked, questioning if my emails were attempting to get things settled before O.B. left.

"Yeah, I wanted things to get better. I wanted to keep my job. I felt like I was threatened and I wanted to fix it if I could fix it."

"He wrote back attempting to smooth it over," Randy said. *"Can you tell me, what was your response or your impression of that response from him?"*

"There's a lot of pieces to this as well, but kind of, like, what do you want? I increased your responsibility. I increased your pay. What are you whining about? There's no reason not to pay you, even though he didn't again. The plan was very subjective and there were lots of ways that they could get around paying commissions at the end of the quarter. And he does ask me to trust him and that we needed to have more communication."

Randy asked, *"Did you have more communication after this?"*

"We didn't have any communication, almost none outside of the monthly calls and email exchanges. When I started getting very vocal about the equality of the pay, he wouldn't even have discussion on that topic."

Randy asked if the way Philippe treated me changed over time, and when I answered the defense objected and the court suggested we take a break, but Randy said, *"Can she finish her answer?"*

"I'm striking her last sentence and why don't you rephrase the question to her and we'll let her answer that," the court advised.

Randy rephrased his question. *"Okay. Tell us the ways in which, without speculating as to what Philippe was feeling, tell us the ways in which Philippe's treatment of you changed over time."*

Before I could answer the defense objected again, requesting to go to the bench to argue this. Instead the court noted that we were at the time of day when it had been agreed that we would break for the day. So the jury was released and I was told I could step down. I would have to wait until the next day to see if I could answer Randy's questions.

- 13 -

TO TELL THE TRUTH

Before testimony resumed each side entered exhibits that had been discussed with the court at the end of the previous day. There were many, mostly consisting of emails and several statistical documents relating to compensation plans. In all, there were 42 exhibits entered for the plaintiff and 69 for the defense. Once all the exhibits had been admitted I was recalled as a witness.

Thoughts lingered in my mind about my previous day on the stand. My lawyers had told me I did okay, but I did not hear the raves I was hoping to hear from them. I thought that maybe they're not telling me I did worse than I think I did. I knew in the back of my mind I was imagining all the horrible outcomes that might happen; I was a mess, taking long breaks between my sentences and trying to compose myself to continue. Often I would be handed tissues because I couldn't stop crying. And, I dreaded Charlie. During his cross-examination I felt like it was very personal between us—I felt like he wanted to hurt me, just like Philippe. But I kept telling myself over and over that I would not let him get the better of me; I would be strong and he would not take me down. In my head I would say to myself, "Bring it on, I will be ready." Thankfully my testimony would begin with Randy asking the question, and that would give me time to become calm before the cross-examination.

Randy began by referring to one of the documents and asked me about my 2007 commission plan. *"Let me ask you briefly about this last paragraph on the terms and conditions. This first sentence says should a conflict exist between any provision of this compensation and your employment contract to which this compensation plan is an exhibit, this compensation plan shall control.*

"Did you ever have a chance to compare the compensation plan against your employment contract?" he asked.

"I didn't have an employment contract," I answered. *"It's something I fought after to include the things like severance and other things that I knew the other managing directors had."*

"You had conversations about that employment contract that's mentioned in your compensation plan?" Randy inquired.

"At least several times, with Philippe, asking him for exactly that. I didn't have an agreement."

Randy then had me look at another exhibit—T. K. Cheung's 2007 compensation plan. He was a peer of mine who ran Asia-Pacific. Randy pointed out that the first difference was that my compensation plan was considered 50 percent base, 50 percent commission. T.K.'s base pay was 60 percent and only 40 percent commissions. So in essence he had more of his salary guaranteed. Additionally, his salary was greater than mine. He also had very lucrative incentives for overachieving targets upward of 200 percent of the exceeded quota—I didn't.

Next Randy presented the plan for the managing director for the European countries. His plan also included an annual car allowance.

"Did you have a car allowance?" Randy asked.

"No, I did not," I confirmed. *"There's also a grant of stock options at the point that he took this position that I was not offered at the time,"* I pointed out.

Randy later questioned, *"The issue isn't whether or not you received them* [stock options]. *The issue here is that Mr. Aminaee received them when he started the job?"*

"Correct, at the point of taking his position," I affirmed.

Randy then referred to the plan for the managing director of South America, a much smaller territory than my North American territory. The plan showed that he made $100,000 more than me just in base salary alone.

"Were you led to believe at the time that you took the managing director position that the terms of your compensation plan were going to be equal to the compensation plans of the other managing directors?" Randy asked.

"Not only was I promised that, I was led to believe because I was running the largest region in the world that mine would actually and could be considered more lucrative than the others. Yes."

Randy returned to the question he had tried to ask me at the end of the preceding day. *"Did some of the ways that Mr. Tartavull treat you change over time?"* he asked.

My answer was rather lengthy. *"Yes, they did. They changed dramatically, I think, once O.B. left in August. I had a bit of a buffer and somebody at least to throw me a life jacket when some of the attacks and some of the things were happening. So that buffer was gone. I had to interact with Philippe more regularly, again, through email, some phone calls. A lot of promises were made. And I think the frustration of talking with him, telling me that he would look into things and then the consistent lack of response to the concerns that I raised, just continued."*

Randy then asked about Philippe not traveling with me to visit customers. Immediately the defense objected, saying that issue had been covered the day before. But the court disagreed, saying, *"I don't remember with Ms. Shipley; I think there's been some discussion about that, but I don't believe she's discussed it yet. You may proceed."*

Explaining that this was hugely important I detailed the reason why. *"For me it was a credibility issue,"* I pointed out. *"There was no announcement from the company when I was made managing director, which is unusual. So the industry really didn't know. So I was trying to validate who I was and the importance of this position. Managing director is a title that a lot of the competitors use. It's well known. It's a very prestigious title in the industry that we're in."*

Relating to Jaime Arroyo's earlier testimony of how Philippe had traveled in all the other countries, I added, *"He [Philippe] was based in Phoenix. We had two major customers sitting right in the backyard in Phoenix, Arizona. And even with them physically located in Phoenix, Arizona, there was no outreach to them either."*

Randy eventually asked me to explain why I believed Philippe's failing to visit my clients contributed to my claim that I was treated differently because of my gender.

"I was left on an island to do this job," I said. *"I had no support from my immediate manager, Philippe Tartavull, to do my job. And the fact that he visited with all of the other managing directors, the fact that he made asserted efforts to meet with them, to meet their customers, to create that foundation and that support, clearly told me that I was being treated differently."*

Next, Randy asked about the Cartes trade show in Paris. Like the witnesses before, I explained its importance, adding how I had made repeated requests to attend. I emphasized that I had inquired as to whether there would be a meeting of the managers and if so, told Philippe that I needed to be there. I said that he had assured me there would not be a managing directors meeting during the show, but that later I found out there had been.

Randy then referred to an exhibit, which was a weekly report I had written to Philippe with my comments in black and his in red.

"Let's talk about his response—what you wrote to him about Cartes," Randy said.

"This is when I put it in writing that I understood that there was a meeting that I was not allowed to attend. One of the subject matters was just critical, which was a whole new line of multi-lane terminals that were being

introduced at the show. This is a unique channel to the United States and almost the United States only and that this whole new line by us was being launched and discussed and created. And I was not allowed to be in attendance at the show or in these meetings."

Randy asked me to talk about my reaction to to Phillipe's statement, *"I got a pulse from the MDs of what they want and the fact is that our priority is to regain share in the U.S.'"*

I explained, *"He, I think, dismisses the fact that there was a formal meeting, number one, and he admits that their strategy discussion on the U.S. territory that I ran and those dialogues happened without me either present or on the phone."* I felt this point was a perfect example of how Philippe had intentionally treated me unfairly and differently.

Wanting to further emphasize the impact, Randy asked, *"Again, let me ask you, why is it that you feel you're being left out of the meetings and Cartes, not being allowed to attend? Is part of your feeling of being treated differently because of your gender?"*

My answer was pretty candid. *"There's no other common denominator. You go through the common denominator theory. My male counterparts were there. I asked to go. Strategic discussions about the future and my region were discussed, and I was omitted. And I think it was a clear attempt by Philippe to cast me aside. I was making my numbers. I was producing. There were no performance issues."*

Randy later moved to a string of emails relating to my request for some calculations to be done on one of my accounts that I should have been paid for in the third quarter.

"I remember expecting to be paid at the close of the quarter," I recalled. *"There would be sales managers underneath me, salespeople underneath them. I personally sold this deal—I closed it, but nonetheless it's still a hierarchy. My manager would have been paid. The sales rep that had nothing to do underneath me would have been paid. So, yeah, I expected to be paid. And when the third quarter closed I was not paid* [for the commissions on the account].

Extensive questioning followed about other accounts, emails that went back and forth because of non-payment issues and a variety of issues that all fed to the unending saga of my being treated differently. At one point Randy introduced another discussion I had with Philippe where I had again asked about an employment agreement.

"*Provide some context to this,*" Randy said. "*It's my understanding the other MDs have this provision.*"

"*Right. I mean I can't even count how many times both verbally and in writing that I addressed this issue with Philippe. This is just another example,*" I explained.

"*I'm really trying to make it clear to him that I knew there were inequities. I knew that the other managing directors were making more money despite the size of the regions. I knew that my package wasn't fair. I knew I didn't have a contract. I knew I didn't have severance. And, I'm begging him to do something about it.*"

"*What's his response?*" Randy asked.

"*That he's tired of these discussions.*"

"*How did you react to that response?*" Randy asked.

"*It was a defining moment. I was pretty much at the end of my rope by this time. I mean I clearly believe that he would never respond to my requests, that he didn't care. It wasn't important to him. I wasn't important to him and nothing was going to change.*"

Randy then read from an email from Philippe in which he said, "I want to have one and only one discussion on this topic when I come back."

"*Did that happen?*" Randy asked.

"*It did not.*"

Randy asked a series of questions about other emails, all of which pretty much covered the same issues but never resolved anything. By this time it was probably no surprise to the jury when Randy addressed the fact that I decided to resign and had sent my letter of resignation to the chairman of the board, Norman Stout. He had me read segments of the letter and eventually asked, *"So in your letter to the chairman of the board, one of the points you made to the chairman of the board is that you were being treated differently as a female?"* he asked.

"I did," I admitted.

"Tell us a little about the date you decided to leave," Randy then inquired.

I explained that for a long time I had been courted by Ingenico, a competitor, and that when an internal memo to the company came out on December 18 announcing that the CEO role would be permanently given to Philippe, it became clear to me that nothing would change.

"On the same day I signed the offer letter to go to Ingenico," I said, explaining that although I had made the decision to leave Hypercom on December 18, I actually resigned on the first Thursday of the New Year.

"So what happened after you announced your resignation?" Randy asked.

"I got a call from Philippe that was short and brief. 'What's going on' (a little panicky). 'I'll call you later.' It was a very brief conversation. 'Is this done? Are you going?' Very short dialogue. 'We'll talk later.' So he hung up."

"Did you talk with Philippe? He said we'll talk later," Randy asked.

"I let him know I was going to a competitor. Standard operating procedure is that everything gets shut down and cut off. They immediately cut your email off, they cut your phone off, so I was prepared to be let go. I was packed. I had all my files in order for the people who would come behind me so I was ready to walk out the door, but that didn't happen. My email kept going and I was told I was going to get a call from Philippe's assistant, asking me to come to Phoenix to have a meeting with Philippe Tuesday after I resigned."

"What was the meeting?" Randy asked.

"I flew to Phoenix. I met with Philippe. He looked at me and said, 'Is this a done deal?' And I said yes. He said, 'Good, go talk to George Ivezaj,' who was in legal. He was an attorney at Hypercom."

"What did George talk to you about?" Randy asked.

"George wanted me to sign a non-solicit agreement for money. I didn't have

a nonsolicit agreement. I could leave. And I believe that the company knew that my staff was very loyal to me. They offered me a nonsolicit agreement for $50,000, some small amount up front and then a larger payment at the end of 12 months if I agreed not to solicit any of their employees."

Randy asked, *"Did you sign it?"*

"I never signed it. I was gracious. I told him I would review it. I took it with me and no, I never signed the agreement."

Then Randy asked, *"Was that your last interaction with Philippe and Hypercom?"*

I explained that it was not because when I left the final quarter had closed and I was due a huge commission check. It was one of the biggest quarters I had ever closed. My calculations were that I was due close to six figures.

I said, *"Emails started going back and forth and I was very much surprised by the fact that I was going through the same battle that I did every other quarter and they were going to find ways not to pay me."*

I explained that there were two big accounts for which they refused to pay me. They claimed that I couldn't be paid on one of them because of an internal term called a "revenue recognition" issue. On the other account, Hypercom had made a decision not to ship the units before the end of the year as ordered so they wouldn't have to recognize the additional revenue in 2007. So they didn't ship those units until 2008 and notified me that I would not be paid for those units despite the fact that I had sold them. The inequity prevailed once more for me because Hypercom did not defer the revenue for all the people underneath me, despite the fact that those people had absolutely nothing to do with the sale. They all received their pay promptly. By explaining this, I had to believe that the jury could see how once again I had definitely been treated differently.

The next several minutes were spent continuing to go over compensation plan issues relating to very specific accounts and addressing details of how different aspects of commissions were calculated. I hoped the jury wouldn't find this too boring. It was a lot of detail for them to absorb.

Randy eventually moved to questions regarding the lawsuit that Hypercom had filed against me. Referring to a specific exhibit, Randy asked, *"Can you identify that document?"*

"This is the complaint and the lawsuit filed by Hypercom against me," I responded.

Randy asked me to tell how I was served with the subpoena for this lawsuit.

"A couple of days prior to being served I understood that both Greg and Bernie had been sued by Hypercom, so I was aware something was going on. I certainly didn't perceive anything like this, but I got a frantic call from my son—I was out of town at the time—telling me that there was a guy in a black truck out front of my house trying to talk to me and asking him scary questions about where I was and how to get with me.

"I panicked and I called Ingenico and I said, I think there's some freaky guy outside my house trying to serve me. And they told me to accept service, so I told my son to tell the gentleman when I would be back."

"Before you saw the complaint, before you even saw what was in it, what was your reaction to the idea that you were being sued?" Randy asked.

"It was unfathomable," I replied. *"I can't even describe it."* The emotion of remembering the whole ordeal brought back terrible memories and I choked up and had to pause and ask for a minute. When I continued, I said, *"I think the thing that stood out the most when I finally got a chance to read it and call Ingenico to describe what was in this document was that Hypercom sued me personally. They didn't sue Ingenico, the company I worked for. They accused me of stealing trade secrets. They called me a liar and a thief and they sued me personally. So this was an attack in my opinion that I had to defend myself against."*

Reading from a part of the document, Randy said, *"It says, 'Upon information and belief, Mr. Frey, Mr. Boardman, Ms. Shipley and others at Ingenico conspired to misappropriate trade secrets and other highly confidential and/or proprietary information from Hypercom both before and after Mr. Frey and Mr. Boardman's resignation.'*

"Do you know who 'the others' at Ingenico are in this complaint?"

"No," I answered.

"But it does mention that Ingenico was supposedly part of the conspiracy?" Randy asked.

"Correct," I affirmed.

"Were they [Ingenico] *named in your lawsuit?"* Randy asked.

"They were not," I said.

"And what did they [Hypercom] *ask for?"* Randy asked.

"They wanted a trial. They wanted a judgment against me for damages for stealing trade secrets," I said.

One by one Randy asked if this included all of Hypercom's fees and costs and expenses, attorney's fees, and punitive damages. I acknowledged "yes" to each one.

"They just wanted to sue you personally for money?" Randy asked.

"Yes," I said again.

Randy then asked what happened to me after I got a copy of the lawsuit.

"Once I gave the lawsuit to my boss there was all sorts of activities with Ingenico. I think the first reaction of Ingenico is to protect the company, which is what they should do to make sure that there was absolutely no truth to the allegations made in the lawsuit against me," I explained.

"My business laptop was taken from me. I had to give them over my email, G-mail, personal sign-on. I never deleted an email in my life, most on my computer business or personal. And they went through everything. I wasn't allowed to talk to Bernie or Greg during this period of time. I wasn't allowed to discuss the case with anyone. And basically I just didn't work for a good period of time while they completed their investigation as to whether any of these allegations were true."

"Were you concerned that Hypercom had essentially called you a thief?" Randy asked.

"Very much so," I said. *"It was the talk of the industry. It was unprecedented. So when it happened I think there was a certain degree of, well, God knows, it*

must be true because nobody ever does this. And so I was questioned. There was a trade show shortly after this that I had to attend and it was the talk of the show where I had to talk to people about what was going on and the lawsuit."

Randy moved to Hypercom's lawsuits against Bernie and Greg. *"Did those complaints make allegations about you?"* he asked.

"Yes. I was named all over both Greg and Bernie's complaint for conspiring with them to ask them to steal trade secrets, and I was accused of knowing that Boardman had a non-compete agreement, all sorts of things throughout both documents."

"Did you ever become aware of any specific evidence that Hypercom had before they filed those lawsuits?" Randy asked.

"No, I was never told anything that they had."

"Has anybody at any time since these lawsuits were filed ever identified to you anything that you did that was improper?" Randy asked.

"Absolutely not."

Randy asked me to look at another exhibit. *"Can you identify that for me please?"*

"This is the dismissal of the lawsuit filed against me by Hypercom Corporation," I said.

"This is a voluntary dismissal without prejudice. What's your understanding what that means?" Randy asked.

"I had to ask what it meant," I said. *"It means that Hypercom has dropped the charges against me. But when they added the words 'without prejudice,' what it means is that they can at any time at any moment continue to investigate me to find evidence that there was truth to the allegations and at any time can reopen this case and sue me all over again.*

"They've never apologized. They haven't stopped. They haven't stopped. This didn't stop anything."

Randy asked how it had all impacted me.

"They attacked me personally. They attacked me professionally. They jeopardized everything that I held in value. They jeopardized my career at Ingenico. They jeopardized a reputation in the industry that I had built for

almost 20 years. They hurt people that I really cared about along with me during these allegations. It derailed me from being able to do my day-to-day job and perform at Ingenico. Up until that point I had four very successful quarters at the company and following this my numbers plummeted. I think that the thing that I just mentioned that is the most devastating of all is that this isn't closed. The fact that they haven't put this lawsuit to rest says that they're still attempting to hurt me. I left the hardware business altogether. I've gone to a company called First Data, who's a customer, in hopes of finding a safe haven to get away from this.

"I'm rocked to the core by all of this. It's been...." Suddenly I was overwhelmed, having to relive the whole painful situation, and I started to cry; I simply had to stop for a moment to calm myself. *"I live and breathe this every day,"* I finally added. *"That's all I can say."* As stoic as I had been, I finally just lost it. But I knew Randy had to go on with his questions, and I knew I had to continue to tell my story, so I did all I could to pull myself together. *"I'm sorry,"* I said. *"Go ahead, I'm okay."*

Pausing a moment, Randy then went on and asked me to describe for the jury how the allegations of discrimination in 2007 impacted me.

I took a deep breath and went on; I simply had to respond from my heart. *"Prior to 2007 I was on top of the world,"* I began. *"I loved the company I worked for. I was the best in the industry. I was at just the top of my game. I was well respected and had a fantastic sales team and loved, loved going to work every day inside and out.*

"The year that I spent working for Philippe, in my opinion, has changed everything about me. I didn't cry as much back then. I'm not the same confident person that I was. The mistreatment has changed me to this day and I don't think I'm going to be that person again. The step back from a career perspective has been huge. I've taken steps back in both of the positions I've taken since I've left. I'm now at First Data. And it's a great company, but I'm doing something so different. And I'm 50 years old. I'm starting over. I have two employees. But I guess I'm just—I'm proud of myself for being here and to fight this injustice and the way that I've been treated by Philippe Tartavull."

I guess Randy decided that this was about as good a place as any to end his questioning. *"I have no more questions,"* he told the court.

Even the court could see what a toll it took for me to relive everything through testimony. *"Do you need a break?"* the judge asked. *"I'm okay, let's go,"* I responded as I braced myself for Charlie's cross-examination.

|||||||||

The first thing Charlie addressed was the email that Randy had asked me about earlier in which I expressed feeling that Philippe had attacked me for North American numbers after only being in the managing director's position for seven days.

"You testified yesterday that Mr. Tartavull did not reprimand the other managing directors like he reprimanded you and did not do it in a public way," Charlie said. *"And this email was an example of the public way in which he reprimanded you. Did I understand that correctly?"*

"There was a difference in the way that Philippe reacted to me and other managing directors," I replied. *"And, yes, I mean, it's not that he didn't correct people, but that there was a clear difference in the way that he typically did it to me."*

In a somewhat cynical tone Charlie said, *"What you're telling us is that he never criticized the other managing directors in the way he criticized you. Did I understand your testimony correctly?"*

"Typically not in the same destructive manner," I replied.

With no more questions about that issue Charlie quickly moved to a discussion about the Cartes trade show. He referred to one of many emails that I had sent to Philippe after finally giving up on attending the show in which I mentioned that I only had one or two small customers attending the show so it did not warrant my attendance. After being continually denied attendance and realizing it was a losing battle, I had written that email in relation to what Philippe had said regarding my customers.

To me it was an example of how the defense took testimony out of context and tried to use it against me.

Charlie also presented and read from emails that I had sent to O.B. about the enormous amount of paperwork Philippe requested. In part, I had written, "*The tasks assigned by Philippe continue to burn up a lot of time that I don't have.*" And in another I had, in part, written, "*I've echoed some of my concerns to you over the phone. There are not enough hours in a day most days to do this job. I'm getting hundreds of emails a day, and just answering them is a full-time job. I have a lot of customers to get in front of and I can't do this with the other workload I've been asked to do.*

"*My entire staff is complaining about this work and the time it is taking away from their ability to sell.*"

Charlie asked, "*You wrote that?*"

"*Absolutely,*" I replied.

Making an assumption, Charlie said, "*And it's fair to say, is it not, after looking at these emails that you did not like Mr. Tartavull's request for data?*"

"*That's not true,*" I denied.

"*You felt like it was taking you away from other tasks that you felt were more important?*" Charlie asked.

"*My primary responsibility was to effect sales and to produce revenue and it did take an impact on that ability,*" I explained.

Charlie didn't like my answer. "*It will be helpful if you answer my question,*" he said with an annoying tone. "*You felt it was taking you away from other tasks that you felt were more important, correct?*"

"*I did,*" I confirmed.

Charlie continued to pick isolated segments out of several emails, each time selecting some aspect that he apparently felt would work against me. I felt he selected content that he believed he could later use to make a negative point. One email he referred to was from me to O.B., and Charlie referenced one specific line where I had written, "I want to get out of dealing directly with him. I report to you."

"*Now, these negative feelings of yours were not directed only to Mr. Tartavull, were they?*" Charlie asked.

"I don't understand the question," I replied.

"You have portrayed the company thus far, it seems to be, as a—for you the perfect place to work except for the presence of Mr. Tartavull, is that fair? We sat here for two days and listened to it. I'm just asking the question."

The question seemed so convoluted, but I answered it. *"It was a great place to work."*

"Except for Mr. Tartavull, in your view, correct?" Charlie sarcastically questioned.

"I don't even know how to answer that," I said. It seemed so obvious to me that I had loved working there until Philippe came along and treated me so differently. I added, *"I mean, I got along with most everybody, yes."*

When Charlie tried to enter the next exhibit Randy requested a bench conference. He pointed out to the court that the next series of emails that Charlie intended to go through were all part of a pretrial conference and that he had objected to them. *"Mr. Wayne is just using this as a character assassination of Ms. Shipley,"* Randy told the court. *"He's not using it to show anything about the relationship with Mr. Tartavull. He's using it for no other reason than to make her look like something she's not."*

Charlie argued that he was entitled to show that I had negative feelings toward others to be able to show that Philippe didn't treat me any differently from anybody else. But Randy continued to point out that Charlie's characterization of what I had said was not actually what I had said about Hypercom being a great place to work.

At one point the judge asked to read the one email Charlie had narrowed it all down to. After reading it he said, *"The objection will be sustained."* Randy had won his fight; Charlie could not twist any more of the email content.

Charlie moved on to conversation about compensation plans. At one point he asked, *"Isn't it true that this delay that you've told us about was in large part Mr. Rawls' [O.B.] responsibility and not Mr. Tartavull's?"*

"Not according to the email communication and the conversations that I had with O.B., that he did what he could and that he escalated it to Philippe and that I was told Philippe was the delay," I responded.

From there on, the exchange became very detailed and often even confusing to me as Charlie moved from document to document challenging my recollections about my compensation and the time period in which I was and was not paid. I'm not sure things were ever completely clear to the jury. Much of it became very confusing to me as Charlie had me go from one page to another in various documents.

Finally, Charlie switched subjects from specific payments to the differences that I claimed between what I was paid and what the other managing directors were paid. He brought in documents with hard-to-read figures for other managing directors and made comparisons of U.S. dollars to foreign equivalents. Even I was confused trying to compare a variety of foreign currencies to U.S. dollars, and I was pretty sure the jury would be confused as well.

Eventually Charlie said, *"Now let's leave that topic and talk about what you told us earlier about your lack of a severance, some sort of severance agreement."*

Before I could respond the court interrupted and suggested that we break for lunch. Charlie agreed, saying that he was only halfway done. *"I think the jurors are probably ready for a break at this point in time,"* the judge said. I know I was ready for a break.

|||||||||

Immediately after lunch Charlie directed me to page two of an exhibit book. *"What I'm going to ask you to look at on page two is the paragraph that you wrote, the first words of which are 'Current comp plan',"* Charlie said.

I acknowledged the place on the page, and Charlie went on. *"And specifically the sentence that I've highlighted which is four lines from the bottom where you say, 'At lunch recently I asked you to consider an employment agreement assuring me protection in the event I were to be let go.' Do you see that?"*

"Yes, I do," I responded.

"Now, when you wrote that sentence you were talking about a severance benefit, were you not?" Charlie asked.

I confirmed that I was.

"And you understand the difference between an employment agreement and a severance benefit?" he questioned.

"I understand they were used—the same term was used to describe the same thing depending on whose agreement it was in," I replied.

"When you say the same thing, what are you referring to, a severance benefit?" Charlie asked.

This was one of the problems I had experienced and it was coming to a head. There didn't seem to be any consistency in procedures or agreements so I tried to explain. *"Some of the MDs had severance in their contracts, which I didn't have. Some of the others had severance agreements in their commission letters. So it was in various places."*

Seeming to ignore the inconsistencies, Charlie, in a somewhat more condescending tone than usual, said, *"What I was asking you was—if you don't know the answer, that's fine—if you knew the difference between an employment agreement and a severance benefit?"*

"I certainly do," I responded.

"Then Mr. Tartavull explained to you, did he not, that in the corporations like Hypercom only the top two or three executives have what are called employment agreements. Do you understand that?" he asked, which didn't really seem to clarify or address the issue.

"I understand that's what he said," I responded.

"You don't believe that to be true?" Charlie questioned.

"I believe that there were things like change of control, provisions, and whatnot in agreements with other individuals," I said.

"Well, then, we can move on," Charlie said, never really resolving the whole issue. Then he caught himself.

"One second," he said. *"With regard to your request for a severance benefit, his response to you in your view was, I'm not going to deal with that. I'm asking you for your recollection. Your view of his response to your request for a severance benefit was, I'm not going to deal with this in 2007. I'll fix it in 2008, correct?"*

"He basically said he wasn't going to do anything about the prior year and that he would think about it again, another promise to consider it again for the following year," I responded.

Charlie then noted, *"Although he told you that he would deal with your request for a severance benefit in 2008, he did award you a stock option in August 2007, correct?"*

I agreed that he had, that at least the company had.

"But it was up to him, was it not?" Charlie asked, wanting to demonstrate that Philippe had given me something.

"It's a combination of things," I explained. *"It's the board of directors approving that stock options be granted and then the president signs the letter; yes, or the CEO signs the letter."*

Charlie then referred to the letter signed by Philippe advising that the compensation committee had granted me an option to purchase shares of company stock. It was another attempt to infer that Philippe had not always treated me badly.

When that issue had been dragged out as long as possible, Charlie again turned to commission issues. For the next several minutes the entire questioning went back and forth about specific accounts and details of how and when commissions related to each. It was definitely a "sleeper" discussion because of all the intricate details. He eventually moved to some questions about the lawsuit against Bernie and Greg, mostly reiterating information that had been discussed previously that brought little new insight.

Then Charlie abruptly moved to how upset I had been when Hypercom sued me personally. *"But you've seen no medical doctors in connection with the emotions and the feelings that you have with regard to those things, correct?"* he asked.

"What kind of doctors?" I asked.

"Medical doctors?" he questioned.

When I said I had seen medical doctors he immediately challenged me, reading from my earlier deposition: *"So you have seen no medical doctors in connection with your claim of emotional distress? Answer: No, I have not."*

"That's correct. That's what it says," I said.

Charlie went on to confirm that I had not seen a psychiatrist, psychologists, or any other mental health professional in connection with my claim of emotional distress, inferring that if I had not sought mental help I must not have really had distress. I was annoyed about the fact that I had sought treatment for heart palpitations but that was being ignored.

Charlie's final question was about an email I had sent to O.B. following an article in the news about the golden parachute given to one of our CEOs when he resigned. The email had been mentioned previously, but Charlie brought it out again, making sure that what I had written was again put before the jury. Then he ended his cross-examination.

Overall, I felt pretty good after my cross-examination. I thought I made Charlie look like a bully and that I did a pretty good job of getting the facts out about my case.

Randy asked to redirect and referenced the exhibit dealing with the last discussed email. *"Let me give you an opportunity to explain the context of that statement,"* Randy said.

"It was just my comments that, you know, with tough times and expenses where they were that key executives were leaving the company. They were given very lucrative packages, very nice severance packages and I had a casualness of obviously about the way I addressed O.B. because of our past relationship. And I said, darn, I wish I could resign and make a paycheck. It's a pretty innocent comment."

"Were you commenting about these individuals [the CEOs]*?"* Randy asked.

"Yes," I clarified.

Randy also asked me about the stock option. *"Let me ask you about that stock price,"* he said.

"Stock price at the time was $5.01," I said.

"Do you have any general recollection what the stock price was around the time you resigned?" he then asked.

"It was around $3, and I had to exercise those options, I think, within 30 days."

"How much money did you realize from this grant?" Randy asked.

"Nothing," I replied.

The only additional thing Randy brought up was a question about T. K. Cheung's commission plan, which had been one of the last plans Charlie had referred to regarding commissions.

"He was allowed up to a 200 percent increase above and beyond his base package and his variable," I said.

"Were you given that?" Randy asked.

"No, I was not," I answered, which brought into focus again the issue of my being treated differently.

With that, Randy ended his redirect and announced that we rested our case. As I stepped off the witness stand I felt a huge sense of relief; it felt like the time I ran the Chicago marathon and actually finished the race. I was so proud of crossing that finish line that I wanted to collapse from sheer exhaustion. That's how I felt as I left the witness stand and retook my seat at the prosecution's table.

Now it was time for the defense to call their witnesses.

- 14 -

DEFENSE WITNESSES
TAKE THE STAND

Immediately after Randy rested our case, the judge called for a 20-minute break. As soon as the jury was excused, Charlie told the court, *"We do have a motion for judgment as a matter of law."*

What ensued next was a lengthy debate from the defense, arguing a somewhat complicated point of law. The defense fought vigorously for it. They knew that if they could get the court's agreement, the ruling would exclude much of the critical aspects of my case, thus it would severely weaken it.

I had filed my Equal Employment Opportunity Commission (EEOC) complaint in Georgia, where I lived. The EEOC transferred the complaint to Arizona, the location of Hypercom's corporate headquarters. The law states that if you are in a state where there is a human rights office, a copy of the complaint is sent to that state agency and the applicant has 300 days from the date of the unlawful practices in which to file the complaint. But, if you file in a state that does not have a human rights office (called a non-deferral jurisdiction), then you must file your complaint within 180 days of the unlawful employment practices.

"There's nothing to indicate that the charge was filed in Arizona," Charlie said. *"In fact most of the record would indicate that for some sort of administrative reason, because Hypercom is headquartered in Arizona, there was some internal transfer by the EEOC of something, and the Right-to-Sue letter was issued out of Arizona,"* Charlie argued. *"But the filing, which is the important act, was in Georgia, so we're within 180 days because Georgia is a non-deferral state,"* he contended.

Charlie then claimed that there had been no evidence to support my charges about the managing directors meeting at Cartes, Philippe not visiting my customers, my not getting severance pay, and my pay comparison to the other managing directors. According to Charlie, we had not been able to support any of the charges. He went on to elaborate on all the areas I had claimed and presented his view of how I had not proved each sufficiently. One by one he continued to cite charges in my suit and do his best to discount them.

What all this meant was that if the judge agreed with Charlie, my claims of not being paid equally and not having an equal compensation plan, and all my other allegations, had not been proven—then the case should be stopped right then.

I had no idea this kind of thing could even happen—that after all my witnesses had testified, the defense could basically contend that parts of our case were not valid to present and, therefore, we had not presented a good enough case to go forward. I was shocked! Suddenly I was scared—very scared. I felt sick to my stomach.

I kept leaning over to David, whispering, "What's going on? Are you kidding me? Could this all be over at this point?" I was becoming a complete wreck. I had come this far and to think it could all end right here was unfathomable. On one hand, I was surprised that my lawyers had not told me about this possibility. But, in hindsight, maybe my lawyers were smart not to tell me of this possibility. Anxiously I listened while David continued to fight to keep my case alive.

When Charlie was finished arguing, the judge said, *"Let me just ask you while you're still on the podium about this argument about the EEOC complaint being filed in Arizona, therefore the 300-day limit.*

"Do you have any authority [law] *to say that does not make the 300-day time limit apply?"*

"I do not have any authority on point," Charlie responded. *"But,"* he continued, hammering his point, *"it was filed in Georgia."*

The court then addressed David. David explained to the court that they had never dealt with Georgia and had only dealt with Arizona. He was firm and confident in his response.

"As you can see from the exhibit, it says Arizona. And, just so you know, nothing happened in Georgia. It was filed there, then it immediately went to Arizona. It was processed and investigated there. We never dealt with the people in Georgia. We only dealt with people in Arizona. So to say that we lose the right of Arizona law in process and procedure, that is just wrong. I mean, it is what it is."

After considerable back-and-forth debate of legal issues David expressed his angst for the defense. *"What they're* [the defense] *trying to do is twist our case and put it into a cubbyhole that we reject,"* he asserted.

Finally the judge was ready to make his rulings. I held my breath, hoping for the best. He allowed some of the minor points for the defense but denied their most critical claims. Most important, he ruled that the case would resume.

My heart raced. I was so relieved. But I was also angry. In all honesty, I don't think the VeriFone/Hypercom lawyers ever expected things to go the way they did. I believe that all along they thought my claims were no big deal. Perhaps now they would realize they could be wrong.

The judge apologized to the jury for the break taking longer than expected, and testimony resumed. Now it was VeriFone/Hypercom's chance to present their side.

||||||||||

The first witness for the defense was Douglas Reich. Now retired, Doug had been senior vice president, general counsel, chief compliance officer, and corporate secretary during most of my employment at Hypercom. Doug is in his late 60s, a little over six feet tall, quite overweight, and balding. He's what I would categorize as a man who thinks very highly of himself—in other words, pompous.

To that regard, it was interesting that the first few minutes of Doug's testimony were spent elaborating on his illustrious professional background. It went all the way back to his early college days, making sure that the jury knew he had an undergraduate degree in economics and a degree in law. He told of how he had spent about eight years with the Securities and Exchange Commission and another 25 years in private practice before going to Hypercom in 2001. He then elaborated on all the dimensions of his work with Hypercom, including his role as corporate secretary, pointing out that he attended all of the meetings of the board of directors.

Charlie put an exhibit on the screen entitled, "Partial Organizational Chart for the Period of April to August 2007." *"What does it represent?"* he asked Doug.

"It represents the board of directors as the responsible body at the top of the corporate chart, and then it shows the hierarchy of responsible people below that," Doug explained.

"Tell us about the situation in terms of Hypercom's business as it existed in the spring of 2007," Charlie said.

"The board of directors had become dissatisfied with the progress of the company and increasing revenue and reducing expenses and, of course, the resulting profitability of the organization, and they weren't real satisfied with the then chief executive officer of the corporation," Doug explained.

"So you were telling us that the board of directors was dissatisfied with the performance of the company?" Charlie clarified.

"Yes," Doug answered.

Doug explained that there were three principal competitors both in the United States and around the world and that Hypercom was a rather distant third.

"Okay. And what did the board of directors do in response to that?" Charlie asked.

"They brought in Philippe Tartavull, who was an existing director, member of the board of directors, and made him president of the company in the spring of 2007. And they empowered him to bring changes to the corporation to increase profitability and improve the company's operation," Doug explained.

Charlie then asked about a dotted line going from Philippe's name to the board of directors. Doug explained, *"That represents the board of directors' unofficial, if you will, direction of accountability and responsibility to Mr. Tartavull."* He went on to say that the board anticipated that the current CEO would be phased out before too long and wanted a more direct chain of command down to Philippe.

"And did Mr. Tartavull make changes when he assumed the office of president of Hypercom?" Charlie asked.

"Yes, he did," Doug said. *"The organization had been a little bit loose, shall we say, in terms of responsibility and accountability, and Mr. Tartavull made people account for their activities in their respective roles within the corporation, judged them by their performance and by their results."*

Charlie asked if Philippe had made any changes in the corporate culture as well. In displaying what I thought was a cocky, smug attitude, Doug responded, *"Yes, he did. As I indicated earlier, it became a culture of accountability. He expected people to perform as he had directed. He expected them to report to him on the progress they were making and if they weren't making progress, why they weren't and how they were going to correct it. He was in effect a breath of fresh air compared to the previous style."*

A breath of fresh air? I thought to myself. From the doubtful look on many of the juror's faces, I wondered if they hadn't had similar thoughts. Only after the trial would I find out that indeed many of the jurors found

Doug's testimony to be quite arrogant, even boastful and condescending.

Charlie went on to address Philippe's impact on the managing directors. *"How were the managing directors affected by Mr. Tartavull and the change in the way that Hypercom was doing business?"* he asked.

Doug painted an unattractive picture. *"Their chains were pulled quite more tightly in that they had to follow the directions that he was giving them. In the past they had operated relatively autonomously without a lot of direct control from above and Mr. Tartavull changed that."*

Charlie asked if Doug had an opportunity to observe Philippe's management style and if so to describe it from his perspective. As you might suspect, his observations were totally different from mine or many of my colleagues.

"Mr. Tartavull is French by nationality. English is his second language. I think that perhaps created a sense of him being a foreigner in terms of most people speaking English," Doug said, obviously trying to establish a cultural excuse for why some people didn't care for Philippe's management style, but that he saw Philippe differently.

"But, his style was relatively sweet," Doug said. With that comment I had to contain myself not to gasp and show my disbelief. "Sweet" would hardly have been a word most people would have used to describe Philippe.

Charlie eventually asked, *"What did the board of directors think of Mr. Tartavull's performance?"*

"The board of directors was very favorably impressed with the change in direction that Mr. Tartavull had instituted and the results that were becoming apparent on a quarterly basis as the financial results were accumulated and published," Doug said.

Doug then confirmed that in July the board also made Philippe CEO of the corporation, but he later testified that a search supposedly took place for a new CEO and the final decision was announced in December 2007. No one ever questioned what seemed to be a discrepancy. As a matter of fact, my lawyers chose not to object or question much of Doug's testimony at all. They were concerned that if they objected too frequently it might seem as though they were trying to prevent Hypercom from presenting their position. So, for the most part, they made few objections, hoping the jury would see through much of the corporate bias of testimony.

Charlie moved to questions about me, asking Doug, *"Did she [Lisa] ever complain to you that Philippe Tartavull was discriminating against her because she was a woman?"*

"No, never did," Doug responded dismissively.

"Did she ever complain to you that anyone was discriminating against her because she was a woman?" Charlie asked.

"Nope, never happened," Doug said rather flippantly.

"As the general counsel, that is, the chief lawyer for the company, were you someone to whom such a complaint could be made?" Charlie probed.

"Not only could, but I would expect that someone would at that level of responsibility," he emphasized

From there Charlie referred to Hypercom's policy manual and also addressed the code of ethics, which Doug said he had prepared along with guidance from outside counsel. He spent several minutes questioning Doug on what an employee should do if they had a discrimination complaint, particularly as it related to human resources, although he did have to admit later that the position of vice president for human resources became vacant in 2006. Doug tried to assure everyone that the human resources department was functioning properly in 2007, despite the fact that there was no vice president to oversee the department.

"The personnel that were within that department were functioning at the same level and the same performance as they had when a vice president had been in charge of it, and that included Betty Seto, who is seated at the table over there," Doug noted, pointing to Betty.

I had to contain myself. I knew that at that time Betty was a clerk with limited responsibility and even less authority. It was maddening that Doug had tried to make her position seem more; it wasn't even fair to Betty.

The next issue Charlie asked Doug about was any differences that he was familiar with among the duties of the various managing directors.

"I became familiar with it because I interfaced with the various managing directors on a regular basis and I understood the directions that came from the board of directors and the chief executive officer and the president to those managing directors," Doug explained.

Charlie then tried to try to convey that because other managing directors worked in different countries with different laws that their duties were different. He ignored the fact that earlier, during my witness testimony, Jaime Arroyo, managing director of Mexico, Caribbean, and Central America, had testified that although there were some different requirements because of laws of each country, that those differences were minor and that the basic duties were the same for all managing directors.

Despite this, Charlie was about to show things differently. He introduced a big chart that Doug had produced that listed each managing director. In a box there were bullet points identifying the specific laws of each country. He then elaborated on each bullet point and its respective requirements for each country.

As an example, he pointed out that severance benefits are required in France and that in Hong Kong there is an employment ordinance that requires employment contracts with all employees and specifies the terms and the severance benefits that would be applicable to each employee. The amount of legal aspects covered became almost overwhelming and, if true, might influence the jury to believe that there were major differences.

The fact was that Doug's overhead chart was somewhat of a sneak attack, if you will. The defense had never provided the document to us prior to trial as they were required to do. We could have objected, but again we did not want the jury to think we were hiding anything or afraid to allow the defense to make claims against us. It did send my lawyers scrambling, however, because later we would have to research all of this to see how accurate it was.

Charlie's last questions dealt with my resignation. Doug explained that the company was concerned that I might hire away some of their employees since I was going to a competitor and this was their reason for offering me $50,000 if I would sign a non-solicitation agreement.

"She did not sign that," Doug confirmed.

"Was it a problem for Hypercom that she did not sign that agreement?" Charlie asked.

Rather smugly, Doug responded, *"Well, it turned out that it wasn't because she didn't hire our employees until about a year and a half after that, so we saved the $50,000 for that 12-month period."*

Charlie then read a segment of my resignation letter, stating, *"It reads, 'The issues that brought me to consider leaving Hypercom are many, but here are the highlights. I asked for financial security to include a severance package since all my peers around the world have been afforded this benefit, yet as a single female Hypercom executive I've been denied this security.' Now, did that sentence cause you concern?"* Charlie asked.

Doug responded, *"No. Because there was no requirement other than what might be negotiated with regard to severance in the United States. And with regard to her peers around the world, the other managing directors, their severance agreements that were in place were required by the local law."*

"Was it your view that Ms. Shipley, in this letter, was disagreeing with the business judgment of Mr. Tartavull?" Charlie asked, trying to make it look like I merely didn't like the changes Philippe was making.

"I think that was in large part what she was suggesting," Doug agreed.

Charlie then referred to another part of the letter where I had written, "The changes I've witnessed in the company are monumental."

"Yes, she's talking about a number of position changes, turnover in executive level positions within the company. In any company there's always going to be

turnover in positions," Doug said dismissively. *"I think she was expressing her disagreement with the decisions that had been made in that regard, questioning the judgment of senior management."*

With that Charlie suggested this might be a good place to end, noting that it was getting close to 4:45 p.m., the time the judge had mentioned earlier as a preferred time to end the day. The court agreed and adjourned for the day and dismissed the jury.

After leaving court I found out that Charlie's entire presentation of the big charts with boxes and bullet points of the laws of each country had thrown my lawyers a real curveball. They had not thoroughly researched all of this information so they weren't sure if any of it was true or whether any of it at minimum was misleading. But they did know they had to find out before cross-examining Doug the next day. Suddenly we had our night's work of research cut out for us.

We all went back to David's suite and Nineveh began the search. She was incredible with research, and her entire efforts focused on finding very specific case law for all the countries—France, China, Brazil, and Mexico. We were up very, very late but found everything we needed. And what we found was gold.

- 15 -

DID THAT REALLY
JUST HAPPEN?

Before court could even begin, the defense was back at it with a new challenge. Apparently frustrated that their dismissal tactics the day before hadn't worked well enough to end the case, they were now going to try to eliminate at least part of my claim. Charlie told the court that he wanted to get clarification on the judge's ruling the previous day as it related to commission for TMS and Best Buy, two large accounts that I had brought in during my final quarter of employment. These were two accounts that Hypercom had refused to pay me commission on despite the fact that they had paid commissions to others who worked for me.

Charlie argued, *"Because there was a voluntary resignation, because Ms. Shipley admitted that she would have been paid had she stayed, that fact coupled with the other admission that two people were paid for those commissions in the first quarter of 2008, [after I, Lisa, had left] that there is no Equal Pay Act claim here with regard to those two commissions."*

Legally, Charlie was trying to make an amendment that might sway the judge to set aside the issue of my not being paid commission on these two accounts because I had voluntarily resigned. But the judge wasn't ready to make a snap decision.

"Let me take that up on our morning break so we can go ahead and get the jurors in here," the judge said, leaving the issue hanging until later. With that, Doug Reich was recalled to the witness stand.

Charlie began his questioning with the topic of Bernie Frey and Greg Boardman resigning from Hypercom. Doug confirmed that the company had been advised by both men that they would resign on the same day. *"And Mr. Frey had admitted that it was a coordinated resignation at the insistence of Ingenico,"* he said.

"How did Hypercom's management react to these simultaneous resignations and the news that these two executives were going to work for Ingenico?" Charlie asked.

"We took it very seriously and were quite alarmed because we were in the process of developing and implementing a new strategy in North America and both Mr. Boardman and Mr. Frey were instrumentally involved in that exercise, and they had confidential information that would be very valuable for Ingenico," Doug stated, establishing a perfect setup for him to justify why Hypercom had sued all of us. The further line of questioning was aimed directly at trying to show that Hypercom's lawsuit had nothing to do with retaliation for my having sued them.

"Are you aware that Ms. Shipley is claiming in this case that Hypercom went to court against Mr. Boardman, Mr. Frey, and her to retaliate against her for suing Hypercom for gender discrimination in this case?" Charlie asked.

"Yes, I'm aware of that," Doug confirmed.

"And what's your reaction to that claim?" Charlie asked.

"It's totally baseless because we brought the actions against Mr. Boardman, Mr. Frey, and Ms. Shipley in order to protect the assets and the business interests of Hypercom. As executives of Hypercom we had a fiduciary responsibility in that regard, and that was totally separate from any litigation that she had brought against us alleging gender discrimination," Doug explained.

"What did Hypercom hope to accomplish in filing these lawsuits?" Charlie asked.

"Well, what we wanted to do was to prevent Mr. Boardman and Mr. Frey from going to work for Ingenico and using the confidential and proprietary information that they had learned and developed at Hypercom for the benefit of Ingenico," Doug explained. Eventually Charlie had to bring up the fact that all the cases were settled. *"So ultimately how was that case resolved?"* he asked.

"Ultimately it was settled about a year later," he said. He went on to make it sound like Greg had actually stolen valuable information. *"Mr. Boardman admitted that he had taken improperly and stolen in effect the Hypercom information, thousands of documents. He agreed that he would either return or destroy those documents and not use them for any purpose other than what was authorized by Hypercom."*

"And there's been testimony in this case that the Hypercom documents that Mr. Boardman stole were of no importance, and then in fact they were returned to Mr. Boardman, is that true?" Charlie asked.

"No, that's not accurate," Doug said defensively. *"The documents were very important."*

I couldn't believe how Doug was twisting the truth, but I also knew that the jury had heard from Greg earlier and knew what really happened.

Apparently the defense was hoping that the jury would believe their twisting of facts, even though they had to confirm that the case against Greg was dropped and that, subsequently, all the other cases were dropped as well, including mine. But Doug had an excuse for that.

"We made the business decision that in light of the Boardman and Frey actions that there was no longer a good business reason to continue that action," Doug explained.

Charlie addressed the fact that their case against me had been dropped without prejudice, meaning they could refile the case at any time in the future.

"Does she have any reason to fear being sued now?" Charlie asked.

Doug's answer stunned me. Although I'm sure he didn't mean to, it sounded like an admission of sorts.

"Not that I'm aware of," Doug said. *"Hypercom was acquired by VeriFone in August of this year. Mr. Tartavull is no longer associated with Hypercom. I know no reason why VeriFone, which now controls Hypercom, would want to bring an action against her."*

Apparently the jury found Doug's answer stunning as well. When he said that I no longer had anything to worry about since Philippe wasn't there, almost every jury member looked absolutely shocked and immediately turned to look at me, as if to say, "Did you hear what he said? Did he just admit that Philippe only did this to get back at you?" It was as if Doug unconsciously admitted that Philippe had filed the suit out of retaliation without realizing what his answer implied. My lawyers had advised me to be stoic at the table, but it was hard to be stoic throughout Doug's obviously biased, and at times false, testimony. So when the entire jury looked at me with shock as they had just done, I would simply shake my head in disbelief.

That concluded Charlie's direct examination. Now it was time for our side to cross-examine Doug. Randy would handle the cross-examination, and little did Doug realize just how prepared he was to do that. We knew that Doug had absolutely twisted the truth in the overhead chart he referred to the day before. In some cases his testimony verged on out-and-out lies. Randy was well prepared to challenge him. Also, throughout Doug's and Philippe's subsequent testimony I had continually written comments about their lies on sticky notes and passed them to my lawyers.

|| | | | | | | | |

Randy began cross-examination by forcing Doug to admit that some of the responsibilities he had boastfully claimed in his testimony the day before were slightly exaggerated, if truthful at all. For example, after asking Doug to refer to his deposition testimony, Randy said, *"I'm going to start with some of your testimony from yesterday. You indicated that you were the chief compliance officer for Hypercom, is that correct?"*

"I did," Doug said.

"And I believe you testified that part of your responsibility was to ensure that employment laws are enforced at Hypercom, is that correct?" Randy asked.

"Yes," Doug responded.

"Now, isn't it true that when you were the general counsel you really didn't have any day-to-day responsibility for labor and employment matters at Hypercom?" Randy challenged.

"We certainly interfaced with the human resources department on a variety of matters involving employment at Hypercom," Doug tried to justify.

With that, Randy asked the court if he could give Doug a copy of his deposition transcript, which he then referred to, pointing out that Doug had been under oath when he gave the deposition and referring to specific pages.

Then Randy firmly asked, *"Were you ever chiefly responsible, and by chiefly responsible notwithstanding that you're the final report, in other words, were you the first report for labor and employment matters at that company or was that handled by other lawyers? Was that your answer?"*

Doug responded, *"My answer was we managed outside counsel with respect to labor and employment matters. We did not have in-house capability."*

Charlie objected, saying that what was read was not an impeachment of the question and answer that had been earlier asked. The judge asked to see the deposition transcript and after reviewing it, overruled Charlie's objection.

Randy continued, *"Isn't it true that you as a general counsel essentially delegated that responsibility to others and merely supervised their work?"*

Doug danced around the answer, and it became extremely clear that he was simply hedging and trying to find ways to justify his earlier testimony.

Randy then challenged Doug's testimony that he had direct dealings with managing directors—in particular me.

"When Ms. Shipley was promoted to managing director, you did not have any direct contact with her, isn't that true?" Randy asked.

"With respect to what?" Doug asked, being somewhat contrary.

"Direct contact with her," Randy repeated.

Again, Doug didn't seem to want to answer, asking again, *"With respect to what?"*

"Did you have any direct contact with Ms. Shipley with respect to any of her duties?" Randy firmly asked, hoping to make his question crystal clear.

Finally, Doug admitted, *"Not that I can recall."*

One by one Randy continued to address every issue of Doug's earlier testimony. One by one as Doug answered, it became very evident that he had exaggerated or embellished the truth in many of his answers the previous day. But the place that Randy really began to challenge Doug was when he began to question him about the PowerPoint chart he had used the previous day, which dealt with the duties of managing directors of various regions around the world.

Randy put Doug's chart up on the big screen. On the chart were listed each country and boxes for each. Each box contained a listing of the different duties that Doug had testified each respective managing director dealt with. He did this specifically to point out that managing directors from other countries had duties that I didn't have for North America.

"You testified yesterday that that was a document that you prepared to assist you with your testimony, or you assisted in preparing?" Randy asked.

Doug confirmed that he assisted in preparing the document.

"Okay. And if I understand your testimony, you said that these were some of the responsibilities of other managing directors outside of North America. Actually, that's the title of the chart, is that correct?" Randy asked.

"The title of the chart is 'Additional Duties of Managing Directors Outside North America,'" Doug confirmed.

"And just as a reminder, you did not supervise any of these managing directors directly, correct?" Randy asked.

"That's correct," Doug said.

"But you were involved sometimes in the contracts, contracts not only as employment contracts, but also the contracts that they were entering into as part of their business responsibilities." Randy clarified. Doug confirmed.

Randy first referred to Kazem Aminaee, managing director who was responsible for France, and pointed out that in the appendix the first sentence of his major responsibilities states, "Identify key markets and customers that hold the largest potential for the company."

"The first major responsibility for Mr. Aminaee was to identify the key markets and customers that hold the largest potential for the company, correct?" Randy asked.

Doug apparently wasn't expecting to be questioned about this. Either he didn't understand or he didn't anticipate being questioned and wasn't sure how to answer.

"I'm sorry. Where are you referring...?" Doug stuttered.

"Identify the key markets and customers that hold the largest potential for the company, correct?" Randy asked again.

"I'm sorry. I'm not following where you're at," Doug said, seeming to be very confused.

"Do you see the column where it says major responsibilities?" Randy asked pointedly.

"Okay. I see it now," Doug finally said.

Randy repeated the question and Doug finally responded, *"Yes."*

"And I assume the potential is going to be the potential for sales or profits for the company, correct?" Randy continued.

Remaining confused, Doug said, *"I'm not...that's the way it reads."*

"Is there anything in the description of major responsibilities that says that Mr. Aminaee has legal responsibilities for subsidiary corporations and must certify the accuracy of audits or tax returns?" Randy asked, referring to duties Doug had attributed to Kazeem and had listed in the overhead chart.

"I don't know. I haven't read through the entire appendix. I don't know. I

haven't read through it," Doug said defensively, still seeming to be caught off guard.

"Did you help draft this contract?" Randy firmly asked. Doug had testified the previous day that he had been involved in all contracts.

"Worked through outside counsel back in 2007 or 8, whenever it was signed," Doug awkwardly replied.

"But I understand you to say that as general counsel that you were responsible for knowing about these duties, that that was part of your responsibility to be aware and familiar with the responsibilities of the managing directors," Randy noted, reading verbatim from Doug's earlier testimony.

"Would you like me to read through the appendix and I'll be able to make that determination?" Doug said defiantly.

But his attitude didn't deter Randy. *"I had thought you would be familiar with the contract. My apologies. Go ahead. Yeah, let us know. Is there anything in this contract on the major responsibilities that says that—well, never mind. There is nothing in there that—unless you point it to me—there's nothing in there that says that Mr. Aminaee had legal responsibility for the subsidiary corporations and to certify audits or tax returns."*

Doug's response was, in my view, rather pathetic. *"I haven't read that appendix for quite some time and I'm not sure that I could say that without having read it,"* he said.

Randy persevered. *"Is there anything in this appendix—this major responsibilities—[that] says his job is to supervise account and finance activities?"*

"Same response," Doug answered.

"You don't know? Anything in there, major activities that says that he is responsible for supervising operations, software application, and development? Same response?" Randy questioned.

"Same response," Doug said again.

"Anything in there that describes his responsibility as supervising regional human resources functions? Same response?" Randy asked.

"Same response," Doug said again.

"Supervise various groups, repair, customer's requests, or manufacturing? Same response?" Randy questioned again.

"Yes," Doug said.

"These will all be evidence for the jury so they consider that, I suppose, if you're not able to," Randy said. *"And, isn't it true, as far as corporate filings go for the subsidiaries, that Hypercom hired a service that prepared most of the filings, and the managing directors really had no other obligation other than to sign their names to those things?"*

As if this wasn't enough to show just how false Doug's earlier testimony had been, Randy moved on to address yet another country, *"These laws in France that are up on this exhibit didn't actually apply to Mr. Aminaee's contract, is that correct?"*

"That's correct," Doug had to finally admit.

The whole scenario was highly revealing, and to make it more apparent to the jury, with every point that Randy covered that Doug couldn't or wouldn't confirm to be accurate, Randy took a bright pink highlighter and dramatically drew a huge, glaring "X" through the point on Doug's chart to clearly emphasize that what Doug had presented was absolutely incorrect. When he had discredited all of the points, Randy drew one huge, bright pink "X" across the entire document. It was right out of a scene from *Law & Order*—brilliantly dramatic and driving home a point. And, it definitely made an impact on the jury. You could see it in their expressions. It was almost as if they were rooting Randy on.

But Randy didn't stop there. He went on to do the same thing with every other managing director's duties that Doug had listed on his chart. One by one he challenged Doug on the inaccuracies for every country, and one by one he continued to mark a big pink "X" through the listings that were inaccurate. The late night research by our team had definitely paid off; we had our facts and Randy did a brilliant job of proving that. By the time he pointed out all of the factual errors, Doug's credibility with the jury was destroyed—it was apparent by the way they reacted as Doug continued to present lame responses.

Randy's remaining cross-examination covered issues regarding Hypercom's lawsuit against me, my two colleagues, and Ingenico. As he drew to the end of his cross-examination, he asked Doug, "*In the process of any of these litigations did Hypercom ever find any additional information that would suggest—any new information that would suggest that Lisa stole confidential information and trade secrets?*"

"*I'm not aware that there were any definitive findings in that regard,*" Doug admitted.

"*And you indicated that the reason that Ms. Shipley should not fear being sued again and called a thief for stealing trade secrets and information is because Philippe Tartavull is no longer with Hypercom, is that correct?*" Randy then asked, making this important point one last time.

"*That was one of the reasons that I mentioned, yes,*" Doug responded.

Randy had been extremely powerful; he had absolutely nailed Doug on all his inaccuracies and embellishments. He was polite enough to never refer to any of them as lies, but he clearly made his point by Xing each and every one of them with the now famous bright pink highlighter.

When asked if he had any redirect, Charlie was quick to say, "*No redirect Your Honor.*"

With that the jury was excused for a well-deserved break and the judge was ready to address the issue that Charlie had brought forth earlier in the morning—the issue of Charlie trying to make an amendment regarding my commission for TMS and Best Buy.

|| | | | | | | | |

After about five minutes of discussion, the judge said, "*I'm going to deny the motion as it stands right now, Mr. Wayne. You may renew it at the conclusion of the case, but you will need to put on that evidence. You put on evidence and I will give further thought to the argument and to what's been presented. I'm not going to allow the amendment of the complaint at this time.*"

This was great news for me. It meant that all aspects of my case would remain as filed and amended by us. We were pretty sure this was now a dead issue because there was very little evidence that Charlie could provide to support his motion. With that good news we all took advantage of the time left in this short break. I especially needed some time to refresh because when we resumed I figured things could get very interesting. Philippe was taking the stand.

|||||||||

I have to admit seeing Philippe after all this time triggered a mixture of emotions. As strange as it may seem, four years later, having to confront him still scared me and evoked a mix of anxiety and fear. I hated that he still made me feel that way. When he took the stand I felt like here I was, David fighting Goliath. I also wondered how he felt given the fact that he even had to be here in the courtroom having to testify. I knew he never expected to see this day come. He had spent an inordinate amount of money, hoping I would just go away. But here he was—forced to face me.

Charlie began his direct examination by having Philippe confirm that he had been president and chief executive officer of Hypercom until August 2011, when the company had merged with VeriFone.

"Are you both a citizen of the United States and France?" Charlie asked. Philippe confirmed that he was and that he lived in Phoenix and California and had lived in the United States for about 24 years. Charlie had Philippe talk about his kids, his education, and just about every job he had prior to joining Hypercom.

As Philippe responded to questions, I quickly observed that he wasn't being his direct, matter-of-fact, unemotional self. Instead, he spoke rather quietly, almost timidly; he was not at all the arrogant, aggressive man that I had known. I was sure his lawyers had coached him. Other than his strong French accent, Philippe displayed little of the person I confronted for ten torturous months.

"When the board of directors hired you to be the president, what did they tell you to do?" Charlie asked.

"Well, they didn't tell me what to do, but they tell me what direction the company should go. The company was one of the three companies in the space. I mean, there was a lot more, but we were the third one with Ingenico and VeriFone. If you look at the performance of the company, we were losing money and our sales have been pretty flat compared to our competitor. And so therefore my mission was to increase the revenue and to put the company back to profitability."

"Did you develop an overall strategy to achieve those goals?" Charlie asked.

"Yeah, in order to achieve those goals there was, I would say, three things that I was focusing on." Philippe began to explain. As he went on I could see that he was trying to establish a logical reason for why he had spent time in the foreign markets rather than mine.

"So, if you think about all the company that sell point of sale terminal, out of a hundred terminals that is sold, 15, one, five, are sold in the U.S. and the rest are sold outside the U.S. which would be 85. And at the time the company was very much U.S. centric," Philippe said.

"What do you mean by U.S. centric?" Charlie asked

"Meaning all the decisions were very much taking in the U.S. and it was clear that there was some potential to develop the company outside the U.S. And so I refocused the attention of the company to try to get in those market outside the U.S., mainly in Europe or in Asia where that's the, you know, the largest market. The second point was we were not doing very well in terms of forecasting and being able to anticipate what would be the revenue for the company," Philippe explained.

"Were the people responsible for developing these forecasts ultimately the managing directors in each region of the world?" Charlie asked.

"They were the managing director and they were also working with our own team in order to develop the forecast. But ultimately they were the people in charge of coming to me with the forecast. And then the subpoint of this was to have a better understanding and a better control of our expenses," Philippe said.

"So when you took over as president what changes did you make in the company?" Charlie asked.

"Well, as I mentioned, I redirected more the focus on Europe and Asia and Latin America. I asked a lot more information on—or forecast we prepare. And I start to have a lot more question on the way we were spending our money," Philippe explained.

"Did you take a more direct role in the day-to-day sales and marketing activity of the company?" Charlie asked.

"Yes, I did. Actually to think about it, we were in the storm. We were losing money. So if you're on the ship, on the cruise ship and there is a storm, you want the captain of the ship to be in charge of the company. So we were a lot more hands on," Philippe said.

"And how did the managing directors react to your taking a more direct role in the day-to-day operation of the company?" Charlie asked.

"There was some frustration with most of the managing directors," Philippe responded.

"In what way?" Charlie asked.

"Well, because I was asking a lot more questions. I was asking more accountability. And I think they were not used to it. And so it take some time before you settle in this change," Philippe explained.

After explaining some of the other changes Philippe had made, Charlie turned the questioning to Philippe's relationship with me.

"Let's talk about your relationship with Lisa Shipley. When did you first meet her?" Charlie asked.

Philippe explained that the first time we met was in 2006 at a board meeting, prior to his being an executive with the company but while he was on the board.

"And when you became Hypercom's president in February 2007, did you learn about Ms. Shipley's prior job performance?" Charlie asked.

"Yes, I did. Like I did for every month, my direct report. I did a people review, what we call a people review, performance review," Philippe explained, adding that he also had input from the current CEO and from

O. B. Rawls. He also explained that he looked at my clients.

"What did you learn?" Charlie asked.

"I know that she was a very good performer. She was extremely good with clients. That was my conclusion," Philippe said.

He's good, I thought to myself. I guess he's going to try to make it look like he thought highly of me and treated me respectfully. At one point he even said that he responded to one of my emails by congratulating me for sales that I had in process. Charlie even asked him about a letter he had written to me in which he notified me that he was awarding me stock options.

"And why was she awarded this stock option?" Charlie asked.

"Because I was pleased with the performance of Lisa."

Charlie continued to reference numerous emails. In each, he selected remarks that demonstrated that Philippe had complimented me.

"Before we move on to another subject," Charlie said, *"let me ask you, have you ever heard the term, quote, 'junior managing director'?"*

Philippe flatly denied ever hearing the term, but when Charlie asked if he ever used such a term, he responded, *"I make a mistake during my deposition,"* Philippe calmly explained. *"I should have used the term 'new managing director.'"* Philippe later added, *"And, by the way, I correct myself during the deposition right away, if I remember."*

I had to bite my lip not to show my frustration at how Philippe was trying so hard to convey that he had just mistakenly used that condescending term when he spoke to the other managing directors about me.

Charlie next referred to an email from me. *"We're going to look on the second page. The paragraph that I've highlighted,"* Charlie directed Philippe.

"It says, 'Philippe, I do not feel as though I've had your support since you've come on board. Circumstances in North America are extraordinary and I believe that you question my abilities to handle the task. If this is the case, let's talk honestly and put our cards on the table. I'm working too hard and too fast

not to have the support of the executive management team of Hypercom.' And, what was your reaction when you read this paragraph?" Charlie asked.

"I was surprise. Because I did feel I was supporting North America like any other region," Philippe said in a very innocent, humble tone.

"Did you feel that you were supporting Ms. Shipley?" Charlie asked.

"Yeah, absolutely, yeah," Philippe replied.

After a bit more discussion about this email, Charlie said, *"Now, let's move on to another topic. Did Ms. Shipley ever say to you that she thought you were discriminating against her because she was a woman?"*

"No," Philippe said dismissively. Then Charlie asked questions about the Cartes trade show—particularly relating to any meetings.

"Were any account reviews done at Cartes in 2007 as it turned out?" Charlie asked.

"We were expecting to try to do some, but at the end of the day because of the show we didn't have the time to do that," Philippe said.

"Did you meet with the managing directors in attendance as a group at Cartes in 2007?" Charlie asked.

"I did, but not with all of them at the same time. I'm not sure I remember exactly because it's far away, but it's my recollection that I think T.K. was still with customer when we tried to do that," Philippe replied. Further questioning to clarify didn't help much. *"I don't remember, you know, the detail of the discussion obviously. But there was no major information. I mean, decision that was taken, and I think the message I was trying to pass over there is to—that in 2008 we would have to put more resource location to North America since we were losing share a little bit,"* Philippe said, seeming to trivialize the whole thing.

"Did Ms. Shipley suffer any disadvantage by not going to the Cartes show in 2007?" Charlie asked.

"Absolutely not," Philippe alleged.

As I was listening to Philippe's testimony I couldn't help but wonder what the jury was thinking because earlier other witnesses had testified exactly what was discussed at the meeting and how it directly related to my North America territory. The discrepancy was so obvious to me, but I wasn't sure it would be to the jury.

"*Now, let's talk about your contacts with Ms. Shipley's customers,*" Charlie said, changing the subject. "*Did you refuse to meet with Ms. Shipley's customers?*"

"*No,*" Philippe replied.

"*Did you meet with any of them?*" Charlie asked.

"*I met with some of them,*" Philippe alleged.

"*Okay. Can you tell me which ones?*" Charlie asked.

This is when Philippe began to lose credibility with the jury.

"*I don't remember, but I think I met with First Data. I think I met with First Data and I may have met with Heartland and I may miss some. It's about a year ago,*" Philippe said with an absolute straight face.

When Philippe said he had met with First Data every member of the jury turned and looked at me in disbelief. They knew this was an out-and-out lie since just the day before the president of First Data had testified that Philippe never met with him. I shook my head in disbelief. I was actually surprised to see the jury react so visibly. For the most part, the jury showed little expression during anyone's testimony. This time they couldn't hold back their shock.

Charlie quickly turned to an unrelated topic; maybe he had seen the jury's stunned reaction to Philippe's totally untruthful response.

After breaking for lunch Philippe continued his testimony relating to questions about compensation and my request for a contract and severance—all areas in which he tried to justify his reason for handling these issues in the ways he did. Although his justifications were nonchalant, I'm not sure how believable he was. To me he was too nonchalant.

"*Okay. Moving to another topic,*" said Charlie. "*Are you aware that Ms. Shipley claims that you subjected her to humiliating treatment at the managing director's meetings and conference calls?*"

"*I am aware now,*" Philippe said, inferring he previously had no awareness of this.

"Is that true?" Charlie asked.

"No," Philippe responded without elaborating.

"Did you ever throw something down in disgust and walk out of a meeting while she was making a presentation?" Charlie later asked.

"No," Philippe said. Again his response was contradictory to the fact that earlier testimony by others had proven that he had walked out.

It hardly mattered what Philippe was asked. All his answers indicated that either he hadn't done what he was accused of doing or he was simply unaware of the situation.

"How did you learn that Ms. Shipley had resigned?" Charlie eventually asked.

"I got an email and then we have a phone call," Philippe said.

"And what was your reaction when you received Ms. Shipley's email telling you that she had resigned?" Charlie asked.

Philippe said that he was "surprised and confused." He went on to explain that he had been planning to give me the severance benefit I had requested, and that he was also considering appointing me to be the managing director for all of the Americas. *"I was thinking about Lisa,"* he said. He even had the audacity to testify that when he talked to me before asking me to come to Phoenix he had said, *"I asked her if there was any way that she can change her mind and also what I was proposing to do regarding the Latin America and the answer was her mind was made up and that she was going to leave."*

"And so did you tell her you were considering her for the position of managing director?" Charlie asked.

"Yes, I did," Philippe responded.

"For all the Americas?" Charlie clarified.

"Yes," Philippe answered.

I could hardly believe what I was hearing. It was all so contrary to what had actually happened and what he had actually said.

Later questioning revolved around the lawsuits that Hypercom filed against me, Bernie, Greg, and Ingenico.

"Did you decide to file these lawsuits?" Charlie asked.

"I approved the lawsuit but it was decided by our legal team," Philippe responded, making it sound like he wasn't the decision maker.

"Did you have any input into who was sued or other details of the lawsuit?" Charlie asked.

"No. Not that I think, we divide the job in two. The legal team was looking at the legal angle of the case and I was looking more on the operational side how are we going to manage the company losing two very important key employees," Philippe tried to explain.

"And in giving your approval for the lawsuits did you consider the fact that Ms. Shipley had this case against Hypercom claiming discrimination?" Charlie asked.

Given the innocence he had portrayed to earlier questions, his answer was no surprise.

"No, it didn't cross my mind because they are two different topics," Philippe said. With that Charlie ended his questioning.

I sat in somewhat disbelief wondering what the jury was thinking and wishing that a more real and candid portrayal of Philippe would come forth during his cross-examination. Philippe had not been believable to me, but I knew this man. The jury didn't. All I could hope was that they had seen through his controlled demeanor and deceit.

- 16 -

GET YOUR FACTS STRAIGHT

Now it was time for our side to cross-examine Philippe. David Ritter would handle this. He began by addressing my commission issue.

"Just before the end of your direct exam you said you did not have any knowledge of commission complaints in the fourth quarter by Ms. Shipley, correct?" he asked.

Philippe affirmed that was right. So David referred him to a specific email that had been part of Philippe's deposition. *"Isn't it true that this email talks about commissions in the fourth quarter with respect to TMS and that she's having an issue with it with Clint Jones and she's copying you on that email, isn't that correct?"* David challenged.

Philippe had to respond. *"Correct,"* he said.

"So you did have some knowledge about fourth quarter commission issues that Ms. Shipley had, isn't that right?" David again challenged.

Philippe had to admit that he had.

David's pushing for truth had only begun. He was about to set the record straight and point out the many ways that Philippe had twisted the truth or simply lied. The next issue David tackled was the retaliation lawsuits.

"You said you relied on your legal team, correct?" David asked.

Philippe replied with a simple, *"Correct."*

"But you made the final decision to file those lawsuits, correct?" David asked, forcing Philippe to agree and even forcing him to agree that he approved them.

"Was it important to you as a CEO of the company that Hypercom win these lawsuits?" David asked.

"It's always important to win if you do a lawsuit, yes," Philippe responded rather matter-of-factly.

"Did you ask your legal team what the evidence was to support the claim against Ms. Shipley that she had conspired to steal confidential trade secret information from Hypercom?" David asked.

Philippe's response was so convoluted and evasive that David said, *"Let me ask the question again because maybe I was not clear."* Then he stated the same question again and once again Philippe sidestepped the issue, not really answering the question.

"Okay. I'm going to try once more because maybe I'm just not making myself clear," David said very firmly. *"I want to know if you asked your legal team, either the lawyers from DLA Piper or Mr. Reich, your general counsel, what evidence, what support there was to show that Ms. Shipley had conspired to take Hypercom confidential business information? I understand your answers up to now, but I'd like you to answer that question for me, sir."*

"I didn't ask these exact questions," Philippe finally admitted.

"Okay. Did you ever come to learn what evidence your legal team had to support a claim against Ms. Shipley personally that she stole or conspired to steal Hypercom confidential business information?" David continued to press.

"The answer from the legal team was that both those senior employees were leaving at the same time to go to work for Ms. Shipley with a large amount of documents that were stolen and this is what we needed to do," Philippe said, again not really answering the question.

But David didn't let up; like a pit bull with a bone he simply pressed on. *"I'm not talking about Mr. Frey and Mr. Boardman,"* he said. *"I'm leaving them out of my question. Okay. I understand that they left on the same day. Did you ever come to learn any information from your legal team to support the claim against Ms. Shipley that she conspired to steal Hypercom information?"*

The defense objected but the court overruled and Philippe had to answer.

"At the time we didn't have 99–100 percent proof, but we are close—very strong suspicions that when you leave a company with all these documents, there will be utilization of those documents," Philippe said.

"And you made the assumption that because Mr. Boardman took information, that Ms. Shipley had a role in that, correct?" David asked.

"No, I didn't make any assumption. I followed the recommendation of my team," Philippe said, again putting it all on his legal team.

David went on to explain that the court eventually dismissed the suit against Frey and said, *"Your legal team recommended to you that they dismiss—that Hypercom dismiss the lawsuit against Ms. Shipley?"*

"Yes," Philippe reluctantly replied.

This entire dialogue should have clearly supported the fact that Hypercom's suit against me never had any substance and was clearly pure retaliation. But, I'd have to wait and see if the jury made that conclusion.

One of the next things David attacked was the fact that Philippe had referred to me as a "junior managing director" during a meeting in front of my peers and again in his deposition. Philippe's excuse was that he had said that in a deposition after six hours and what he had meant to say was that I was a new managing director. When pressed about the actual time he had been in deposition, Philippe said, *"I don't remember how many hours, but it was after a period of time."*

Not letting his answer go unchallenged, David told Philippe that he could see his reference on page 42 or 43 of the deposition. Then he hit Philippe with some time reality.

"That didn't take six hours to get to, did it? That's kind of near the beginning of your deposition, right? Would you agree with that?" David said, referring to the actual deposition.

Being faced with reality, Philippe's response was simply, *"I guess when you're in deposition time it seems longer."* Despite his trying to dismiss its importance, I thought it became quite clear that Philippe's reference to me as a junior manager had definitely happened and that it was no accident.

To demonstrate just how evasive Philippe's earlier testimony had been David next went to a part of his deposition where he had stated that he wanted to make me president of all of the Americas as a managing director.

"Just give me a month and a year, in 2007, when you made that decision," David said.

"It was in my head between September and December, and I make the final decision during the break," Philippe said.

"Is there a single company document that indicates that you wanted Ms. Shipley to become the managing director for North and South America?" David asked.

"No. Because most of the time when I do reorganization, which is what I was planning to do with the acquisition of TASQ, I was thinking about how to organize the company. I do that for myself, and I don't have this document going around in the company. That wouldn't be the appropriate thing to do," Philippe explained.

Just to see if Philippe would stick to his original claim, David said, *"I just want to make sure that there's not a single company document that supports your thought process that she should get that position. Am I correct in that?"*

"The reason I'm thinking that is I may have draft for myself some document, so I don't know if they exist now or not, but I don't think I communicated that outside to anybody. That I'm pretty certain," Philippe said, wavering a bit from his original adamant position. At that moment I thought the jury

may be beginning to see how many of the things Philippe had said may not have been quite the way it really was.

David then questioned Philippe on other issues including my comp plan and request for severance. He eventually brought up the subject of gender discrimination by referring to an email I had sent to Philippe in early December.

"Did you believe that this email that Ms. Shipley wrote you on December 1st and which you responded to twice on December 2nd was a complaint of gender discrimination to you?" David asked.

"I didn't understand it like that, no," Philippe responded.

"Prior to Ms. Shipley resigning did you ever believe she was complaining about gender discrimination?" David asked.

"No," Philippe said.

David then had Philippe refer to an exhibit. *"This is something we have seen before. This is the email that Ms. Shipley sent to Mr. Stout as part of her resignation. You've seen this before, correct?"* David asked.

Seeming to hedge, Philippe said, *"I saw it now, yeah."*

"Well, have you seen it before today?" David asked to clarify.

Philippe admitted, *"Yes."*

"Okay. You saw this document—this email about the time Ms. Shipley resigned, correct?"

"I don't remember if it was exactly in January. I may have seen it later. I don't remember the date I seen this email," Philippe said, beginning to hedge again.

To refresh Philippe's memory David read part of my email to him. *"The issues that brought me to consider leaving Hypercom are many, but here are the highlights: I asked for financial security to include a severance package since all of my peers around the world have been afforded this benefit. Yet as the single female Hypercom executive I've been denied this security."*

Then David asked Philippe if he would agree that Ms. Shipley's peers were the other managing directors around the world. Philippe's responses were somewhat mind-boggling.

"Define peer," Philippe said. *"What do you mean by peer?"*

"Peers, equal in the company. Do you understand what the word 'peer' means?" David asked in somewhat disbelief.

"Yeah, now that you defined it, yes," Philippe said.

"So would you agree with me that Ms. Shipley's peers in the company were the other managing directors?" David asked.

Philippe agreed and David continued, *"And they were all men in 2007, correct?"*

"They were men, but bound by the legal law of the country in which they reside," Philippe said. He didn't realize that this very issue had been disproven the day before. Thus that excuse was not very effective.

David then referred to my resignation letter one more time. *"In summary, I believe I have been handcuffed to do my job effectively. I've asked for simple things to do my job well, financial security equal to my peers, and I was denied,"* he read from evidence.

"When you read this for the first time did you believe that to be a complaint by Ms. Shipley of gender discrimination?" David asked.

"As I told you, I was surprised and confused," Philippe responded, avoiding the point of the question.

"So, is the answer no, that you didn't think this was gender discrimination?" David pressed.

"No. I was just surprised by the tone of the letter, yes," Philippe said.

It was clear that Philippe was simply going to continue to act naive about anything related to gender discrimination. But, David had done a good job of making a point that Philippe hadn't treated me in the same way he treated my peers.

A considerable amount of the next questioning dealt with my commission plan, its delay and as a result the delay of my getting paid. Following that were questions about the Cartes trade show. At one point Philippe tried to infer that I had asked if I needed to go to the show rather than simply asking to be able to attend.

"Is it your testimony that that is the only time that she asked if she could go or had to be there?" David asked after Philippe inferred that I hadn't made a big deal about going.

"I don't remember," Philippe hedged. *"But we have meeting, another conversation, I cannot tell you that now."*

"Isn't it true that you told her she could not go because of costs, it was too expensive?" David asked.

After avoiding the question directly and talking about bringing people from all parts of the country, Philippe finally said, *"No. It was a combined reason, a customer first and obviously the additional cost."*

Philippe said that I had only a small amount of customers and therefore I didn't need to go.

"If Ms. Shipley wanted to go to Cartes would you have let her, or would you have said, you don't have enough customers and the cost is too high?" David asked.

"I don't know," Philippe responded.

"Well, Mr. Tartavull, I believe you told me earlier that as early as September you were considering Ms. Shipley to be the managing director of both North and South America, correct?" David reminded Philippe. Then it got quite interesting as David began to build a web of questions that didn't bode well for Philippe.

"Is it your testimony that you had made a decision to promote Lisa after Cartes?"

"I think it was in the December time frame that I came to this conclusion," Philippe said.

"But prior to Cartes you were thinking that Ms. Shipley may be the managing director for both North and South America, right?"

"I was thinking about it, yeah," Philippe responded.

"And even though you were thinking about that you didn't think she needed to be at Cartes, correct?"

Philippe now got a bit defensive. *"Look, going to Carte, it's a 16-hour flight back and forth,"* he said.

"How much?" David asked.

"Okay, it's a time difference," Philippe agreed. *"By the time you go and you come back, you lose a week. We were at the end of the year and there was no specific client there and we were trying to increase revenue. I didn't think it was—and other decision was that she didn't want to go because she didn't have any major customer. If she become the managing director of Latin America, she have plenty of opportunity to go visit those customers in the region. I don't think it was critical at this point in time."*

But David reminded Philippe that he had told him that November and December was a very slow time for sales for their business. Philippe's response was rather weak. *"It's slow to—it's not—there is a difference between going to visit a customer at a very high level and just trying to push the normal sales in the different channel that we have. So it's a very busy day-to-day activity."*

"So it was your view that Ms. Shipley's time was better spent in the United States at the end of the year—at the time of Cartes instead of being at Cartes?" David asked.

On that question, Philippe said "no," that it was the managing director's decision and since I didn't have any customers I decided I didn't need to go. Then David referred Philippe to an exhibit marked 2007 Cartes meeting schedule.

"If you look at the second page of this exhibit on day two, Hypercom was having a three-hour cocktail reception, right? Do you see that from 7:30 to 10:30 p.m.? Do you need help Mr. Tartavull?"

After Philippe fumbled around trying to find the page, David asked, *"Did Hypercom have a cocktail party? Customers came? Potential customers? You were there? Other managing directors were there?"*

Philippe admitted there had been a cocktail party, he was there, but he just couldn't remember which managing directors were there.

"And throughout the conference you and the managing directors met with Hypercom customers?" David asked. Philippe agreed that he had

but he couldn't remember if he had met with customers with any of the managing directors.

"You said there was a company called TASQ, and TASQ is a distributor for First Data. And First Data is the largest customer in the U.S., right? And First Data is Ms. Shipley's client, right?" David asked.

"Correct," Philippe responded.

"Wasn't it true that Ms. Shipley was in 2007 also in charge of sales in Canada?" David asked. Then he began to name specific Canadian clients, and one by one Philippe couldn't remember whether they were there or not. Throughout the whole line of questioning Philippe did his best to remain controlled by responding dismissively with short, one-word answers of "yeah, yes, correct, okay." It was quite apparent that Philippe was not comfortable with David's line of questioning. But his evasive responses did little to support his rationale for not allowing me to go to Cartes.

After a short break Philippe returned to the stand for more questioning and David asked him about a meeting that was scheduled at Cartes. He referred to Philippe's deposition in which he had downplayed the meeting to the point where he had said, *"I don't remember who was at this meeting. I don't think it was three hours. I think we were attempting to do three hours, and everybody was late, so I don't remember the exact time."*

"And if I recall your testimony on direct, you don't really recall what was discussed at that meeting?" David asked.

"It was nothing important discussed in this meeting that would impact strategy of the company," Philippe said dismissively.

"So you don't recall any of the managing directors making presentations at that meeting about the state of the quarter in their region?" David asked.

"I don't remember that, no," Philippe responded, despite there being earlier testimony from two managing directors that they had each made presentations.

David then moved to a series of questions related to the importance of the president visiting customers.

"Isn't it true that in 2007 you did not visit a single customer with Ms. Shipley?" David asked.

"No, that would not be true," Philippe said with a straight face. *"We visited customer when we were at ETA* [a trade show in the U.S.] *and I visit—I think I visited First Data with Ms. Shipley."*

"You believe you visited First Data with Ms. Shipley?" David asked, being stunned that Philippe would say that. Just the previous day the president of First Data had testified that he had never had a visit from Philippe.

"Yeah, and we met with Ed Labry [the president of First Data]," Philippe confidently replied.

"With who?" David asked to be sure he heard him right.

"Ed Labry," Philippe repeated.

Again, every jury member turned to look at me in disbelief. They obviously suspected Philippe may be lying; they had just heard Ed Labry testify the day before.

"Ed Labry?" David questioned again.

"Yeah, and I don't remember if he was—he was not in Atlanta, so he was in another city," Philippe said.

"But other than at ETA, it's your testimony that the only customer you visited was First Data?" David clarified.

Philippe then named a few other customers that he thought he'd met with. David followed up by referring to an email that I had sent to Philippe listing the names of clients I felt he needed to meet face-to-face with me. The list included First Data and all the others that Philippe had just said he had met with.

David showed Philippe the list and asked, *"Is it your testimony that you visited First Data and Heartland?"*

"Yes," Philippe answered.

Then David asked, *"Isn't it true that you didn't visit any of those other customers on that list?"*

"I think I met with Motorola," Philippe responded, avoiding the real question.

"Let me rephrase the question because I was inartful," David said humbly. *"Did you visit those customers with Ms. Shipley?"*

"That I don't remember," Philippe responded.

"Did you visit any of the customers under number seven with Ms. Shipley?" David asked, referring to the email.

"I believe I visit First Data. I believe I visit Heartland. I don't remember if it was with Ms. Shipley. I don't remember exactly the one with Ms. Shipley and the one without Ms. Shipley," Philippe rambled. As if Philippe hadn't dug himself a deep enough hole with his answers, David returned to the issue of Philippe meeting with Ed Labry.

"What do you recall—how long was that meeting?" David asked.

"I don't remember," Philippe said.

"Do you remember anything that occurred during the meeting?" David asked.

"No. Not of importance," Philippe said.

Looking at Philippe sitting there, so confident and so unaware of reality, I couldn't help but think that he had no idea that he had just been caught in a string of lies.

It was the perfect place to end and that's exactly what David did. *"Nothing further,"* he said. I guess Charlie decided not to make things any worse. He decided there was no need to redirect.

|||||||||

The next witness called by the defense was Clint Jones. Clint had served in many positions at Hypercom through the years, but his role during my last year was that of chief operating officer for the Americas. He was the guy Hypercom was relying on to cover all the compensation information. Our compensation plans were very complex, made up of a variety of formulas. Clint knew from working with me that doing forecasts and working with the many number variables was one of my weaker areas. But fortunately, understanding numbers and complex formulas was one of Randy's greatest strengths, and Randy was the lawyer who would be handling Clint's cross-examination. I was worried that the complexities of comp plans Hypercom would present might be so new and confusing to the jury that they might simply zone out trying to understand them. But, I also knew that when our turn came to cross-examine Randy would likely make things crystal clear. When it came to numbers, he was a wizard.

Charlie began direct examination by going over all the positions Clint had held at Hypercom, his education, all the information to establish his credibility. Finally he asked, *"Let me ask you some questions about Lisa Shipley. How long have you known her?"*

"Since I was involved in the North American operations roles both as the director and the vice president," Clint explained, later confirming that that would have been since about the year 2000.

"How would you describe the role—your relationship when the two of you were at Hypercom?" Charlie asked.

"Friendly, professional. We got along," Clint replied.

Later Charlie asked, *"After Ms. Shipley was promoted to managing director did she ever come to you for advice?"*

Clint said that I occasionally came to him for advice, noting that I had particularly come to him about forecasting.

Charlie then referred to a string of emails between Clint and me about forecasting and asked, *"Was this forecast process one of Ms. Shipley's strengths?"*

"Probably not, no," Clint responded.

"Did you consider her to be a numbers person?" Charlie continued.

"No," Clint replied.

"And how did Mr. Tartavull react to that?" Charlie asked.

"He was pretty tough on anyone that didn't have their—wasn't a numbers person or on top of their numbers," Clint said.

I figured all of this dialogue was a predecessor to the actual charts and numbers that would probably be presented. I also supposed Charlie would eventually guide the testimony to make the point that I wasn't treated differently. I admit I just didn't quite get it when it came to numbers.

Charlie then asked, *"Did you ever see or hear Mr. Tartavull single out Ms. Shipley for disrespectful treatment at any of these meetings or conference calls?"*

A quick "no" from Clint ended that conversation and Charlie moved swiftly to my compensation plan. For the next several minutes the entire line of questioning revolved around charts filled with columns of numbers and discussion about U.S. dollars and the exchange rates for various countries. It was certainly not one of the most interesting segments of testimony, nor was it the easiest thing for the jury to follow.

After this line of questioning Charlie moved to questions about the commissions I had claimed I had not been paid, commissions on the accounts I had closed during the fourth quarter before resigning. To justify not paying me for those accounts, complicated information was cited about compliance with the Sarbanes–Oxley Act. Clint talked about how accounting under Sarbanes-Oxley was governed by principles, and that these principles included rules about credit limits, so that anything above set credit limits for this specific customer could not be recognized as revenue until that credit limit was either cleared or raised. Thus, until the credit was at a particular point, I couldn't be paid commission. And, since I had left by the time that the credit issue was resolved, Hypercom did not owe me any commission. Yikes! The whole conversation was full of tedious details, and given that I was confused by it, I'm sure many of the jury members were as well.

"So what did that mean for Ms. Shipley?" Charlie asked Clint.

"It means it wasn't in her numbers and her revenue calculations for 2007, so it wouldn't have been included in the calculations of her commissions," Clint said. He later added, *"She wasn't employed at the time we did recognize the revenue."*

"So as a result she was not entitled to the commission?" Charlie asked.

"Correct," Clint affirmed.

"And if Ms. Shipley had been working at Hypercom in the first quarter of 2008 would she have been paid that TMS commission?" Charlie asked.

"Yes," Clint responded.

When questioned about the commission on Best Buy, Clint advised that a significant portion of the order wasn't shipped in the fourth quarter of 2007 and therefore rolled into the first quarter of 2008.

"And why wasn't it shipped in the fourth quarter of 2007?" Charlie asked.

"We didn't have the product built," Clint said, confirming later that if I had not resigned I would have been paid this Best Buy commission in 2008.

I knew that there was another side to this as well as all the confusing information in the commission charts, but the jury would have to wait and hear how Clint would respond to cross-examination.

|||||||||||

Randy hit hard from the very beginning. And in his hand was the trusty pink highlighter.

"Mr. Jones, we've just heard some testimony from you about the compensation plans for all of the managing directors in 2007."

"Yeah," Clint responded.

"But isn't it true that you were not familiar with the 2007 compensation plans of the other managing directors other than Lisa Shipley?" Randy asked.

Clint rejected the statement saying that was not true. So, Randy referred Clint to a page of his deposition transcript and said, *"I'm going to read the question to you that you were asked, and you were under oath at the time of this deposition as well, is that correct?"*

Clint agreed.

"Okay. I'm going to read starting on line 18. 'In 2007 in your role were you familiar with the compensation plans of each of the managing directors?' What was your answer?" Randy asked.

"Not each of them. No," Clint read back.

"Were you familiar with some of them?" Randy questioned.

"Yes, or I was familiar with one," Clint noted.

"Okay. And whose was that?" Randy asked.

"That was Lisa's," Clint said.

Randy went on. *"You mentioned you didn't set the targets—the targets or the payouts, so let me just get some clarification on what exactly your role was. You didn't set any of the base salary for any of the compensations—for any of the managing directors in 2007, is that correct?"*

"No," Clint responded, indicating that he didn't set the targets.

"Okay. And you didn't set the amount of incentive compensation they would get for any of the revenue—hitting their revenue targets, is that correct?"

Clint confirmed that he wasn't involved.

"So you weren't involved in deciding how much someone was compensated for hitting revenue targets, correct?"

Again, Clint agreed.

Randy then went on to confirm that Clint had assisted in preparing the document that showed the numbers of all the different managing directors from around the world—the same document he had so tirelessly used to point out all the exchange rates and how they impacted the numbers. Clint confirmed that he had assisted in preparing the document.

Referring to the document, Randy said, *"Well, let me talk about this earnings side. I don't see anywhere on the earnings side where anybody—where there are any taxes taken out on any of the earnings side for Mr. Asis, is there?"*

"I don't see it now," Clint said. With that Randy marked a big "X" across the box containing that information. You could almost see the jury's reaction—oh great, here it comes, more pink "Xs."

"Now isn't it true that on this compensation chart none of these other managing directors, none of those numbers reflect after-tax compensation?"

"I'm not a 100 percent sure, no," Clint responded. Once again Randy drew a big pink "X" over those boxes, making it dramatically evident that the defendant's numbers were incorrect.

Randy then pointed out that some of the managing directors' compensations were listed with taxes and some without; therefore, the numbers were not equal comparisons. In one instance, they had actually compared my before-tax income to another managing director's income after taxes, all of which Randy pointed out as he drew big pink "Xs" through.

Randy then had Clint turn to another exhibit. *"That is the 2007 earnings statement for Lisa Shipley, isn't that correct?"*

"Yes," Clint replied.

Randy noted that all the payments listed were prior to April 1 of 2007, a period of time when I had not yet been promoted. *"So is it fair to say that compensation did not relate to compensation that was paid to her as a managing director?"* Randy asked, pointing out that numbers were used that were not equal comparisons since at that time I was not being paid as a managing director. *"I would say that's a fair statement, yes,"* Clint confirmed. Wham. Another big pink "X."

Holding onto the now famous pink highlighter Randy pointed to the chart and said, *"So, this exhibit doesn't actually reflect the compensation that was paid to Ms. Shipley as a managing director for 2007, does it?"*

Client seemed reluctant to say "no," so he said, *"Technically, yes, there's some rollover from 2006."* But in reality, the exhibit reflected commissions paid to me before my promotion as well as commissions paid to me once I became a managing director. Once again using his pink highlighter, Randy pointed to the numbers and challenged their accuracy, revealing how the numbers failed to reflect my real fourth quarter payments for 2007. All Clint could do was agree.

Next, Randy referred to a part of the compensation formula that Clint had talked about regarding the need to partially reduce expenses. When asked if I had met that objective, Clint seemed confused.

"I asked if she had partially met the objective," Randy said. *"She had gotten partially there. She reduced expenses?"* Randy asked.

"She reduced expenses. Yes," Clint responded.

"So, under the comp plan it says that she should have been paid on a prorated basis, isn't that true?" Randy asked.

"Correct," Clint said.

"That money was never paid to her though, was it?"

"No," Clint admitted. Again Randy marked a big pink "X."

"So as early as March 16, 2010, Hypercom has known that they did not pay Ms. Shipley under her 2000 compensation plan, is that true?" Randy asked.

"For that specific item, yes," Clint responded.

"And do you have any reason—do you know why they haven't paid her that money?" Randy asked.

"No," Clint had to admit.

With that Randy put a giant "X" through the entire document to signify that the whole exhibit was just plain bogus.

When Randy finished cross-examining Clint it was quite clear he had discredited much of what had been presented by the defense. And once again, he made his point perfectly clear by underscoring all the inaccuracies with the ever-present pink highlighter.

|||||||||||

The defense's final witness for the day was Tai-Kei Cheung, more commonly known as T.K. He had been the managing director for Asia-Pacific during my time as managing director. He was still working for Hypercom, but after the merger with VeriFone he moved to the corporate offices in Phoenix and became vice president of global quality and security. I'm not sure how good a witness T.K. was for anyone; I definitely wouldn't have considered him a strong witness. The defense questioned him about his relationship with me, to which he said, *"It was professional. I also treated Lisa as a friend and confidant."* But there was little he said that supported the fact I had ever come to him as a "confidant." He was asked about compensation plans and duties and, of course, the Cartes trade show. I was disappointed by how different his attitude was about my not being there as compared to two other peers who had testified earlier. But then again, he was there as a defense witness.

"Did Ms. Shipley miss any important Hypercom meetings at the 2007 Cartes trade show?" Charlie asked him.

He simply responded "no."

He gave the same one-word answer when asked if he ever saw Philippe treat me disrespectfully. And when asked what kind of a boss Philippe was, he said he was a "tough boss," with the implication that Philippe was simply tough on everyone.

Charlie didn't ask much more and ended his questions with, *"Did you ever see or hear Mr. Tartavull treat Ms. Shipley unfairly in any way?"* T.K. simply said "no." That was it from the defense.

When Randy cross-examined T.K. he set out to clear up some testimony by others earlier in the day that was a bit misleading. For example, he asked T.K. about his offer letter when he became managing director, a topic that defense witnesses had earlier said was written a certain way because of strict country ordinances.

"And that offer letter included some severance provisions in it for you, is that correct?"

T.K. responded "yes."

"Okay. Were those severance provisions the exact same provisions that were required by the Hong Kong ordinance?" Randy asked.

"Not exactly. No," T.K. responded.

"Were they generous?"

"They were more than generous," T.K. said.

"And, they included, for example, that if the company let you go they would relocate you back to the United States?"

"That's what I negotiated before I went out there," T.K. said.

"You asked for that?" Randy asked somewhat naively.

"Yes," T.K. confirmed.

"And negotiated it and they gave it to you, is that correct?"

T.K. confirmed that Hypercom had complied with his request. That made the point that what I asked for and couldn't get, T.K. had gotten easily.

Randy also asked him about Philippe traveling all the way to the Asia-Pacific region to meet with clients, and again T.K. confirmed that he had done that. At the last moment Randy approached one more issue.

"You testified that you never had an experience of a delay in your compensation as a managing director except in 2006. Was there a time in 2007 that you had to sit down with Mr. Tartavull to discuss one of your MBO targets [managing by objective] *and whether or not you made that target?"* Randy asked.

"Yeah, I had to explain to Philippe because he had just only come on board because he wasn't there in 2006, and it was the previous year [that] *followed that held up my payment for the 2006 MBO,"* T.K. said.

"So he sat down and met with you?" Randy asked, in a tone that conveyed, Really, he took time to sit down with you to discuss this face-to-face?

"Yes, we went through each of the MBOs and which one I had achieved, which ones got delayed until 2008. For instance, one of the ones was the acquisition of the Australian company," T.K. revealed.

Randy seemed to be pleased with this piece of information and ready to end, so he said, *"Thank you."* But T.K. continued on.

"And the other one was the—was one of the customer deals that we had to delay because I was working on a different project at the time."

"I got to back up just one second," Randy said. *"I didn't understand you. Are you saying this talk that you're having with him—I want to focus on the comp plan that it relates to."*

"Yeah," T.K. said.

"Was it related to your 2006 compensation plan? Or was it related to your 2007 compensation plan?" Randy asked to clarify.

"It was related to the 2006 payout," T.K. said.

"Philippe Tartavull had taken over by that time?" Randy asked, somewhat surprised by what T.K. was saying.

"*Yes,*" T.K. confirmed.

"*In early 2007?*" Randy asked again to clarify.

"*Yes,*" T.K. said.

"*And he sat down with you and worked out a compromise related to those issues?*" Randy probed.

"*Yes,*" T.K. confirmed.

Well, if T.K. did nothing more, at least he showed that Philippe took time to help one managing director and that was more than I could ever get him to do with me. Randy ended his cross-examination.

T.K volunteering the last bit of information was unexpected, and apparently it was unanticipated by the defense also. They chose not to redirect. With that the day's testimony ended and the jury was released for the night.

Once the jury had left, the judge advised the lawyers that he had prepared a draft of jury instructions and wanted the lawyers to look them over before morning. That meant that the next day would likely be THE day—the day the trial would end and the jury would deliberate and render a verdict. Just thinking about that moment conjured up all sorts of emotions. On one hand I felt excited, confident, and anxious; I felt we had presented a lot of evidence over the past week that had clearly shown I had good cause for claiming gender discrimination. But then suddenly my mind would shift and doubt would creep in. Was I too close to it all? Could I be missing something because I knew the witnesses so well? Had the jury really seen and heard what I saw and heard?

- 17 -

IF YOU'RE GOING TO LIE, AT LEAST BE CONSISTENT

To say I was nervous as I entered the courtroom this day would be a huge understatement. If all went as planned, this would be the day the jury would come to a decision; that fact alone made me feel anxious, yet excited. After nearly four years I was about to hear from a jury of my peers whether they believed that I had been discriminated against.

There were three witnesses left to testify for the defense. My hope was that their testimony would be shorter than those before them so we could move on. If not, this could drag out into another week. Plus, there was the possibility that I might be called back to testify. Randy and David were pretty sure things would wrap up today, and the judge had prepared both legal teams for that reality. So Thursday night, even though we were exhausted from the long day, our team got together and strategized how to best close the case. How would we sum up five long days of testimony? What were the right words to say to the jury? And, what about the pink highlighter that had become a powerful visual for Randy? Then there were all the untruths—particularly those from Doug Reich and Philippe. Randy struggled with how to handle those. He realized that some were out-and-out lies, but being the good guy he was I knew Randy was also reluctant to be that blunt, that it was just his nature to always take the high road. I'd have to wait until the very moment to see what he decided. But first, I'd have to endure the testimony of three more witnesses.

The first witness called by the defense was George Ivezaj, who had been Hypercom's assistant general counsel at the time that I resigned. Victoria Bruno handled the questioning for the defense. She began by establishing that George reported to Doug Reich, who had testified earlier. Then she asked, *"Do you know Ms. Shipley?"* And when George confirmed that he did, she asked, *"What kind of a relationship did you have with Ms. Shipley?"*

"I would say it was friendly," George said. *"We didn't socialize outside of the office except for one dinner."*

"Did Ms. Shipley ever complain to you that Philippe Tartavull was discriminating against her because she was a woman?" Victoria asked.

George responded "no" and also confirmed that he had never heard from any other source that such a complaint had been made. But when asked, *"Did Ms. Shipley ever complain to you about Mr. Tartavull?"* George responded, *"Yes."*

"In what ways did she complain?" Victoria asked.

"She complained about Mr. Tartavull's management style. She felt that he was pushing the team too hard, that Mr. Tartavull didn't understand the North American market. She didn't like the new commission plan that he was implementing for 2008, and she complained about his accent, that is was thick and hard to understand."

Victoria then wanted to know how George found working with Philippe.

"Mr. Tartavull was difficult to work for, but he was a good boss. He was very demanding. I mean, we have to understand that this was a big change in what the managers and the team had saw [seen] from the management team. He was holding people accountable. He was getting into the details. It was a

big difference from the previous management team where it was very hands off," George explained.

"Based on your conversations and your working with Ms. Shipley during 2007, did you come to a view as to how she was handling this new management style of Mr. Tartavull?" Victoria asked.

"Not well," George bluntly said.

Once again Hypercom was putting witnesses on the stand who clearly wanted to convey that Philippe's treatment of me was nothing different and nothing personal, that he was just doing his job.

Questioning then shifted to questions about why Hypercom filed their lawsuits against Greg, Bernie, and me. Regarding Bernie and Greg both resigning at the same time, George said, *"I think it showed a coordinated effort and an agreement between Ingenico, Mr. Frey, and Mr. Boardman to have them leave at the same time."*

"Was that a concern for you?" Victoria asked.

"It was. I think it was troubling to have the top U.S. salesperson and the top U.S. marketing person leaving at the same time under the direction of Ingenico. These were two people that were key in the North America strategy in how we were going to move the new products forward," George explained.

Later on Victoria brought me into the equation. *"You mentioned that you learned that there was continuing contact between Ms. Shipley and Mr. Boardman and Mr. Frey after she left and they were still at Hypercom. Did you conclude anything from that fact?"*

"I—we concluded that Lisa was the principal reason that Ingenico wanted to hire them and she recruited both of them," George said.

"At the time of your investigation did Hypercom consider the possibility of filing a lawsuit in response to what was happening?" Victoria asked.

"Yes," George confirmed.

"When you and Mr. Reich were considering whether to go to court and file these lawsuits, did the subject of Ms. Shipley's lawsuit against Hypercom for gender discrimination come up?" Victoria asked.

"No," George claimed. *"These were two unrelated events. Ms. Shipley's discrimination claims against the company had nothing to do with the fact that Ingenico had coordinated the resignations of two of the top North American people from the company. Her discrimination claim had nothing to do with the fact that Mr. Boardman had a non-compete that expressly prohibited him from working at Ingenico. It had nothing to do with the fact that Mr. Boardman stole thousands of documents,"* George rather defiantly explained.

Of course none of this explained why Hypercom had sued me personally. But Victoria seemed to be pleased with George's testimony and concluded her direct examination.

Randy began his cross-examination by asking George, *"When Ms. Shipley resigned from Hypercom she had a meeting with you where you presented her with a non-solicitation agreement, is that not true?"*

Victoria immediately objected but the court overruled and George had to confirm that he had indeed done that.

"She never did sign that agreement, correct?" Randy asked.

"Correct," George confirmed.

"So you were aware that there was no contractual or legal restriction on Ms. Shipley from trying to hire employees away from Hypercom, was there?" Randy asked.

George reluctantly responded, *"She didn't sign the agreement, no."*

Randy then approached the whole issue of Hypercom suing me personally. *"And correct me if I'm wrong, but I didn't hear anywhere in your prior testimony on direct, you didn't tell me anything about any knowledge that Ms. Shipley had stolen any trade secrets or confidential information from Hypercom, is that correct?"*

"I didn't testify to that, no," George admitted.

With that, Randy ended his cross-examination. I was saddened by George's testimony. I liked George and I thought we were friends; I didn't think he would back Philippe the way he did. We had talked privately about Philippe and I had told him how I felt I was being treated. Did he really not remember? I was truly saddened to think that he could turn on me in this fashion.

Next on the defense lineup was Betty Seto. Betty held an administrative position in the human resources department at the time of my resignation; she wasn't in a major decision-making role and I had no interaction with her. Since I left and Hypercom had merged with VeriFone, Betty had apparently moved to the position of human resources director, so my assumption was that Hypercom felt she was a viable witness to bring in.

"What were your responsibilities?" Victoria asked Betty, relating to her role before the merger.

"They were the typical human resource administrator functions dealing with pay, recruiting, benefits, and employee relations issue between employees," Betty said.

"We've heard that the human resources department in Arizona was without a vice president in charge in 2007. Do you recall that?"

"Yes," Betty responded.

"So who did you report to during 2007?" Victoria asked.

"The chief financial officer, Tom Liguori, and then the president, Philippe Tartavull," Betty said.

"During 2007 did you know Ms. Shipley?" Victoria asked.

"Yes, I did," Betty said, explaining that she had first met me when she joined the company in July 2004.

"Ms. Shipley has testified that she did not go to the human resource department with her complaint of discrimination because there was no vice president of human resources and she didn't think that you and Ms. Natoli were qualified to handle the discrimination complaint against Mr. Tartavull. What is your response to that testimony?" Victoria asked.

"First, we were qualified. And if we would have received such a claim we would have immediately went to Doug Reich, who is general counsel and also chief compliance officer and got him involved," Betty said.

"If Ms. Shipley had a complaint about Mr. Tartavull's treatment of her would you have wanted to know about it?" Victoria probed.

"*Yes,*" Betty replied, adding, "*because it's part of my job to help the company respond to such claims of discrimination and conduct an independent investigation to protect both the employees and the company.*"

With that Victoria had no further questions and David began cross-examination.

"*How long have you been in the human resources—doing human resources professionally?*" David asked.

"*Now over ten years,*" Betty responded.

"*In your experience in HR have you ever had an employee come to you and complain about discrimination but didn't say—but just explained what was happening to them and not use words such as gender discrimination or race discrimination or sex discrimination? Have you ever had that situation occur?*" David asked.

Victoria tried to object to the question but the court overruled and Betty's answer was pretty revealing. "*Not that I recall, no,*" she said.

David's final question was also telling. "*It's my understanding there's been testimony that there was human resource training in 2008, correct?*"

"*I believe so, yes,*" Betty said.

"*There was none prior to that, was there?*" David asked.

"*No, there wasn't,*" Betty admitted.

That ended David's cross-examination, but he had clearly made the point that only after I had left and filed my lawsuit had there been any kind of HR training. Victoria did her best to try to recoup from any damage David's questioning might have made. In redirect she said, "*Mr. Ritter just asked you about training in 2007, and you said that there was no training in 2007. But what were the employees required to do in the 2007 period which is relevant here?*"

"*All employees were required to sign the acknowledgment of the handbook and the code of ethics that they understood, and that document page got filed in their personnel file,*" Bette explained.

"*In the code of ethics in the employee handbook that you just referred to,*" *do those documents address the subject of discrimination in the workplace?"* Victoria asked.

"Yes, they do," Betty responded.

Apparently, Victoria felt David had made a pretty strong point and did her best to try to overcome it, but the reality was that reading the employee handbook certainly wasn't the same as providing specific training.

|||||||||||

I thought it was odd that the defense brought in the next witness. Dan Diethelm was a board member, and there were only a couple of occasions during the whole time that I reported to Philippe that I had even encountered him. The only time I had any significant conversation with him was December 2007 when I had attended the company Christmas party. I knew I was going to be leaving Hypercom but I hadn't said anything to anyone yet. I went to the party because it would be the last time I'd get to see everyone—sort of my own private "good-bye" time, if you will.

At that party I spoke to Dan, and one of the things he said to me seemed strange. He asked me if I knew a particular woman who worked in our industry. I wondered why he had asked me about her. It wasn't until years later when I saw that woman and approached her that his question made sense. I was shocked to find out from her at that time that Philippe had been interviewing her for my job while at the same time professing to be supporting me. And even all these years later he had the audacity to say he was actually thinking of promoting me. I thought it would be interesting to see what Dan had to say considering the facts.

Charlie conducted Dan's direct examination, first confirming that he had been chairman of the board of directors in 2007 and that he had led the search committee involved in the decision to bring Philippe on as interim president. Dan described the rationale for bringing Philippe on board, and Charlie asked, *"So why was Mr. Tartavull a good choice?"*

"Philippe had come from what I would call a related industry. He was in a business that manufactured the actual credit cards. He knew some of the same customers. His background was sort of in revenue generation, sales and visiting customers and things like that. And so we just thought that that would be a good complement to Will Keiper [the CEO at the time]," Dan explained.

"Did the Hypercom board of directors tell Mr. Tartavull what the board expected him to do?" Charlie asked.

"Yeah, I think everybody—we knew where we were and what the business was lacking and so everybody had those conversations and everybody knew what we needed," Dan replied.

"Did you leave it to him to decide how to do it?"

"Yeah. Directors should be directors and not managers and we left—we set specific goals and objectives and where we wanted to be and where we thought we should be moving relative to our peers. And it was up to them to implement those and get that done," Dan said.

Dan further explained that the company had continually been underperforming and decided to part ways with the current CEO and to elevate Philippe.

"So as of July 2007 Mr. Tartavull was the president and the chief operating officer?" Charlie asked. [Technically, he was interim president.]

"Correct," Dan confirmed.

Charlie shifted the focus. *"Let's talk about Ms. Shipley. How long have you known her?"* he asked.

"I've known Ms. Shipley since I first went on the board," Dan said, confirming that that was in 2001.

"And what type of relationship did you have with her while she was at Hypercom?"

"Lisa was a good executive. We had conversations at board functions. We'd have conversations in the period when I was chairman at management committee meetings. I would assume our relationship was, you know, open and we had no problem communicating with each other," Dan said.

"Did she come to you to talk about issues within the company?" Charlie asked.

"Yes, she did," Dan confirmed.

"Did Ms. Shipley ever come to see you about that search for the CEO?" Charlie asked.

Dan responded *"yes"* and went on to say, *"During the period where we had this management committee, as well as the search going on, when I was out at the office Lisa pulled me aside and wanted to talk about the search and see how it was going. And we spent some time, and during that conversation what she said was that if we made—promoted Philippe to CEO, that she wouldn't want to remain with Hypercom and that she would quit."*

"What was your reaction to that?" Charlie probed.

"My reaction was twofold. First of all, I didn't—she was a good employee and a valued employee and I didn't really want to see that happen, but second of all, because we were running a search and we had to get it right, I wanted to know why," Dan explained.

"What did she say?" Charlie went on.

"She told me several things. She told me that Philippe was—his style was abrupt. She didn't think he understood the market or the customers and that she didn't—that she just didn't think he was ready to be a CEO," Dan said.

"And did she say that Mr. Tartavull was discriminating against her because she was a woman?" Charlie asked.

"No, she did not," Dan said.

"Did she say that he was treating her differently in any way because she was a woman?" Charlie pressed.

"No, she did not." Dan confirmed, adding, *"This is very clear to me for a specific reason. We had—the board of Hypercom had made a change to Chris Alexander, then made a change to Will Keiper. And we were at that point where both financially, as well as the shareholders, we couldn't make a mistake. And when Lisa came to me and said, look I don't think Philippe should be CEO, it raised all sorts of flags of why and I had to ask very specific questions why. I*

had conversations with the other members of the board, told them specifically what Lisa's concerns were. And it was very important not to mess it up," Dan elaborated.

"What specific questions did you ask her in following up on what she said?" Charlie asked.

"Trying to get at specifically what the reasons were and were the reasons that she didn't like his style or she didn't like how he—what his expectations were or how he was trying to change the culture of the company, or were they problems of him doing inappropriate things or violating policies or violating sort of a moral standard or something like that. I wanted to be very clear that there was a difference between he was being tough and changing the culture of the company versus he was trying to—you know, he was doing something inappropriate," Dan claimed.

"And what was her answer when you asked these questions?" Charlie asked.

"She told me that those—the category of issues relating to inappropriate behavior or anything like that wasn't the issue. It was his style and his expectations and his understanding of the market and things like that," Dan said.

When Charlie asked if Dan was surprised to hear that I had resigned, he replied, *"When I got a call that she had resigned, I wasn't surprised at all. She did what she said she was going to do."*

Wow. He sure remembered things very differently, I thought to myself. I guess it was now a case of he said, she said. But I was quite confident that I would have a chance to tell my recollection later when I would retake the witness stand for our final rebuttal. When David did his cross-examination of Dan he did get a chance to probe a bit more and create some doubt.

"You clearly remember that conversation with Ms. Shipley?" David asked.

"Clearly," Dan responded.

"There's no doubt in your mind that it occurred?" David continued.

"None," Dan said confidently.

"Great. After that conversation you felt no need to have any conversation with anyone at human resources, did you?"

"I did not have any conversation with anyone in human resources," Dan admitted.

"And you didn't talk to Doug Reich [Hypercom's general counsel] *about your conversation with Ms. Shipley, either, did you?"* David probed.

"No, I did not," Dan confessed.

David then referred to an exhibit that had my email to then chairman Norman Stout resigning.

"And Mr. Stout did not circulate this email to the other directors?" David asked.

"No. I remember getting a call from Norman saying she quit. But, if he did, I wouldn't remember. I don't remember he did. But, I mean, he may have, but I don't remember receiving it," Dan replied with less confidence.

"You don't remember receiving exhibit 77?" David firmly asked.

"Correct," Dan said.

"This meeting with Ms. Shipley that you recall so well, do you recall when that meeting occurred?" David pressed.

"It was in the summer of 2007, and it wasn't a scheduled meeting. She just pulled me aside when I was in the building," Dan replied, sticking to his story.

"Okay. Do you recall where that meeting took place in the building?" David asked, not letting up.

"I don't remember exactly where. I mean one of the offices in the section where we had board meetings and there was some spare offices in there," Dan said, rather unconvincingly.

"Okay. How long did that meeting last?" David continued.

"Fifteen minutes," Dan said.

With that David concluded his cross-examination. He had certainly created a bit of reasonable doubt, but it did leave things hanging a bit for the jury to determine who was telling the truth.

It was now only mid-morning but it might as well have been midday. Perhaps I was just restless knowing the jury would soon begin deliberation. But we weren't done yet. Randy decided to recall me to the witness stand.

|||||||||

"Ms. Shipley, do you recall having a conversation with Dan Diethelm in the summer of 2007?" Randy asked.

"I do not," I replied.

"Did you ever have a conversation with Dan Diethelm?" Randy questioned.

"I did," I replied.

"When was that?"

I explained that I had met with Dan at the Christmas party. *"The Christmas party was on the 15th. I sat down with Dan and told him everything that was going on in an effort not to talk about myself so much, but to make sure that the foundation was laid for the folks that I was leaving behind. I was very concerned about some of the things that were being implemented for my sales team and my staff and I wanted to make him aware of the issues that I was concerned with before I left, and that was the extent of the conversation,"* I said.

"Now did Philippe Tartavull tell you on the day that you resigned that he was planning to promote you to managing director of the Americas?" Randy asked.

"Absolutely not," I advised.

Switching topics Randy then said, *"Let me just ask you if that testimony were true, that Philippe said he was promoting you, would that have been a position you would have been interested in?"*

"Absolutely. I mean, I had Canada as a market, but getting a more global position would be something very interesting to me and something that I would want—would want to have further dialogue on, yes," I said.

"How would that position, if [it had] been offered to you, have compared to the position at Ingenico?" Randy asked.

"*Well, the position at Ingenico, to be clear, was not a managing director position. Chris Justice, who you met, was president/managing director of Ingenico. I took a step back. I was senior vice president of sales and marketing for Ingenico, so it was not the same position,*" I explained.

"*So if you had in fact been offered a promotion like that that would have at least been something that you would have considered?*" Randy asked.

"*I think the whole notion is completely ironic. I mean, I've had this very incredible year with a man that's put me in—on an island and left me to sink or swim, didn't support—didn't provide any support to me. And the notion that he was—you know, that with this isolation and with this treatment that in his mind he had some great future plans for me is completely ridiculous. But to answer your question, if Philippe Tartavull had not been discriminating against me and offered me a position of running the Americas, I absolutely would have accepted the position,*" I said.

With that I was excused, and shortly thereafter the jury was excused for a 20-minute break while the judge spoke with the attorneys about the final aspects of the trial. When court resumed it would be time for each lawyer to present summations. Soon it would be up to the jury to decide— Was I discriminated against, had I been paid equally, had Hypercom sued me personally out of retaliation?

Talk about nerves intensifying. Soon the outcome I had waited nearly four long years for would be in the jury's hands.

- 18 -

THE END NEARS

As the court convened the judge addressed the jury. *"Thank you for your patience. The break was a little longer than I anticipated, but now we are ready for closing arguments. Because Ms. Shipley has the burden in this case, Mr. Grayson [Randy] is entitled to go first, and if he would like, to reserve time for rebuttal. So he will be allowed to address you first and last, and he's indicated he does intend to reserve time for rebuttal. So, at this time I ask you to give your attention to Mr. Grayson as he delivers his closing argument on behalf of Ms. Shipley."*

As Randy approached the podium he held in his hand the now-famous pink highlighter. He began by greeting the jury, then said, *"Margaret Atwood, the novelist, once wrote, 'We still think of a powerful man as a born leader and a powerful woman as an anomaly,'"* emphasizing that even now, in the 21st century, some still believe there's a difference between men and women when it comes to equality in business.

"Today in my closing I want to talk to you about three things: What you've heard, what we'd like you to do about it, and why this is important. Lisa Shipley came here this whole week to tell you her story and it's a story with an

ending that you will write. So, let's talk about the cast of characters that you saw." Randy then summarized all the people who had voluntarily come to testify on my behalf. Then, to counteract Hypercom's suggestion that I hadn't been discriminated against and merely didn't like change, Randy said, *"Lisa's life was all about change. She relocated to Atlanta, a single mother of three, took over a joint venture and helped integrate Bank of America's credit card processing business. She started all over again at Hypercom. In her 12 years at Hypercom she had a meteoric rise. Lisa knew all about change at Hypercom, and she lived it.*

"Chris Alexander, former CEO, told you Lisa was the best salesperson he ever had. Based on her revolutionizing of this ISO market, Chris nominated Lisa for the industry-wide Movers and Shakers Award. She embraced change one more time in 2007 by taking on the new role of managing director for North America, a role with more responsibility—so she thought—higher pay—so she thought—and more prestige—so she thought.

"What went wrong? Despite Lisa being put in charge of the largest revenue-producing territory in the world, she was paid less than her peers. We showed you the records. We showed you the contracts that Hypercom had and they were clear." Randy then referred to Hypercom's commission charts, which had glaring mistakes that included comparing my pay with taxes to other managing directors (MDs) without taxes.

"Now, is this really a surprise? I mean, we know women have traditionally had to fight hard to be compensated at the same level as their male peers. We know that. The only thing you see in this case is that gender discrimination and pay permeates every level in corporate America. Lisa in 2007 had every right to think she had made it to the top. Why wouldn't she think that? But this case is a lot like a glass ceiling type of case. But the difference for us is that for Lisa, it turned out to be a glass wall.

"You heard how once she made it into that managing director club she began to be immediately shunned by the new president, Philippe Tartavull. Jaime [Arroyo, former Hypercom MD for Mexico], *I think, put it best saying Philippe's treatment of her was more destructive rather than constructive. And*

that's what Lisa told you. Philippe took away her confidence. He didn't treat her like a managing director. He treated her like he accidentally said in his deposition, like a junior managing director.

"We heard that not only was Lisa's compensation plan unfair, it was untimely. And you saw that once it was finally approved, Philippe immediately cut her commission by $10,000 from what had been agreed upon.

"Lisa was working for two and a half months as a managing director with a promised raise that didn't come. How would you feel? Would you feel appreciated? Would you feel like you were being treated fairly if you had to beg, beg your boss for a raise that had been promised to you? Is that fair?

"Then you saw that it happened again almost right away. Almost as soon as the second quarter closed she, and only she, had to wait one more time when her compensation was questioned. And Philippe's email response was exactly what O. B. Rawls told you his [Philippe's] attitude was—hey, I gave you a raise. What are you complaining about? What's the big deal?

"Lisa told you in the fourth quarter it was raining orders. It was a record quarter. And then even though she was making record sales for Hypercom, things were unraveling for her terribly.

"You hear all this evidence that Lisa was not compensated fairly. And Hypercom will say to you, yeah, yeah, things get delayed, we got to look at things, what's the big deal. But you also heard evidence directly from T. K. Cheung, Jaime Arroyo and O.B. Rawls that none, none of the other managing directors had this problem. They were all paid timely. Their commissions weren't questioned, delayed, deferred, or denied every quarter. Look at the payroll records.

"You heard her say that Philippe never visited with any of her clients even though he went around the world to travel with the other managing directors. Philippe said, hey, I was busy. What's the big deal? But you heard Ed Labry tell you how important it was that he have a relationship with the president of the company that he buys millions of dollars of product from annually.

"You heard about Cartes, the international trade show. Hypercom says, she didn't want to go. What's the big deal? But you heard Lisa explain that.

You heard her explain exactly every email you see on this subject that they're making a big deal out of, that they say, no big deal. She said, you told me there would be no planning meeting. Why did you leave me out? Philippe's response by email, oh, all we did was talk about your territory for the next year. What's the big deal?

"*You heard him say yesterday there was no real meeting, but then look at the schedule that's right there, three hours of meetings.*"

|| | | | | | | | |

"*Now, Hypercom has said to you, no. Wait. She never said the magic words 'You are discriminating against me on the basis of my gender.' But, I don't know what else you can make of statements like, as the first single female executive I was denied this, or I'm not being treated the same as my peers, who Philippe begrudgingly admitted were the male managing directors. Then you hear Betty Seto tell you that in the ten years as an HR person she's never heard a complaint from an employee about discrimination that wasn't worded exactly, I am being discriminated against on the basis of my gender or race.*

"*You saw that December 2nd email from Philippe himself. You even heard his testimony. Lisa called it the lightbulb moment. And Philippe even said, hey, I'm finally trying to figure out what she's saying. And he finally got it right. You read it yourself. I am not treating you the same as the other managing directors with the comp plan, et cetera. Uh-huh. And then finally, as you heard, Lisa chose to resign after Philippe was made the permanent CEO of Hypercom. That ought to be where this story ends, but it's only the beginning.*"

Randy next brought up the whole issue of Hypercom's lawsuit against Bernie, Greg, and me, pointing out that Hypercom's general counsel, Doug Reich, tried to explain away their reason for filing the lawsuits by saying that Bernie admitted that his and Greg's plan to leave was all coordinated with Ingenico.

"*Did you see how Bernie reacted to that? This is a guy that told you, I don't like to lie. And when he was asked about that, did you see him? His lips quivered. He punched the desk. He said, that is absolutely not true. I believe Bernie.*"

|||||||||

"*You heard a lot of untruths and half-truths from Hypercom in this case, but let's focus now on the lawsuit against her and the allegations Hypercom made about her in the Frey and Boardman suits. She says that Hypercom was motivated to file frivolous claims against her to retaliate for her gender discrimination lawsuit that she filed against Hypercom. Now let's focus on some evidence. You heard that a lawsuit of this kind was unprecedented. Unprecedented. You also heard it from the Arizona court. Read that opinion. It's in evidence. And I want you to focus in on what they accuse Lisa of doing. That's the point of our case. You've heard from Hypercom's witnesses all these stories about what Greg did or what Bernie did. I think we've proved that even those reasons are a bunch of hogwash.*

"*Hypercom sued Lisa personally for money damages. They called her a thief even though Dough Reich couldn't even tell you how they've been monetarily damaged. They didn't sue Ingenico. They sued Lisa.*

"*You heard Greg Boardman talk about how after his lawsuit kept going on, Hypercom kept using his lawsuit to dig for more dirt on Lisa. Look at the settlement agreement. It's in there. The main thing they wanted from him [Greg] was sworn testimony that they could use in another case. Which case? This one. He told you in the interview he was forced to go on [that it] seemed the whole focus was on Lisa Shipley. If you had any doubt that they were really not interested in the so-called confidential information, why did they give him back the same material that they made such a big deal out of?*

"*You heard Doug Reich and Philippe and George all acknowledge that they were aware of Lisa's lawsuit when they decided to sue her personally. You heard that the architect of the strategy is the very same law firm that was defending Hypercom then and today, DLA Piper.*

"*Here's what you haven't heard. Not one, not one single plausible justification for why it was necessary for Hypercom to sue Lisa, not one; not one good reason for why they called her a thief and kept calling her a thief, not one. And it's not just me talking. Read the Arizona court order requiring Hypercom to pay attorney's fees because they had made allegations in bad faith against Ingenico. Go to the paragraphs that are referenced in that court order and you will see that they relate directly to what Hypercom claimed Lisa did. And the Arizona court said those allegations were bad faith."*

||||||||||

"Now I need to spend a few minutes talking about the case that Hypercom put on for you. I'm going to call this the pink highlighter of falsehoods." With this, Randy began making huge pink checkmarks as he checked off specific points on the overhead document.

"You heard Doug Reich try and convince you that the reason Lisa was not given a severance benefit was because Hypercom was just trying to follow the laws of the respective regions. How'd that testimony work out for them? You already knew this, but in case there was any doubt, T. K. Cheung put the nail in the coffin of his own truthfulness. He told you that those severance agreements had nothing to do with what the legal requirements were." Check.

"You heard Doug Reich tell you about the different duties of the managing directors and how the four managing directors had different duties. Look, if the testimony of O. B. Rawls, Lisa, Chris Alexander, Jaime Arroyo, and T. K. Cheung wasn't enough to convince you the managing directors' jobs were the same, read Kazem's contract. It's right there for you." Check.

"Then later on in the case you heard Clint Jones try and explain how Lisa made more money than many of the other managing directors. Remember that chart? How did that work out for them? Hypercom has the nerve to ask you to compare one person's after-tax take-home pay with everybody else's pre-taxed pay so that they can show you that they really did pay Lisa more than Reinaldo Assis, after-tax versus pre-tax. Are you kidding?" Check.

"Now, let's talk about Philippe Tartavull. He told you some big whoppers. He tried to come off like some big know-it-all, but unfortunately for him he didn't sit here all week like you did. When he tried to tell you that, oh, yes, I did have a meeting with Ed Labry and Lisa Shipley, First Data, you knew—you knew from the moment the words left his lips that it was a lie." Check.

"And when he tried to tell you the other managing directors had severance benefits and that was because it was to conform with the laws of the other countries, you knew—you knew as those words were leaving his lips it was a lie." Check.

"And let me ask you, after all this time do you really believe that if Philippe had told Lisa on the day that she resigned he was going to promote her to president of the Americas, give her a severance benefit, if he had told her that for real, do you think this case would be here? You know there's a reason that not one single document exists to substantiate what Philippe wants you to believe that he was planning to do in this alternate future that never came. You know this—it was a lie." Check.

By now the jury was looking at a list filled with huge bright pink checkmarks that dramatically pointed out all the untruths that Hypercom's lawyers had presented. It was very dramatic. Hopefully, it had also made a solid impression in the jurors' minds that would bring them to the conclusions we all were seeking.

"One of the things that I think is important for you to understand when you get the judge's instructions is that you have the right to infer from all of these falsehoods that Hypercom is covering up. They are hiding to cover up their discriminatory retaliatory motives. Their inability to be honest with you, their attempt to put one over on you is reason enough to enter a verdict against them.

"It's hard to put a value on the damages, but we trust you to do that. You're going to have the right to award punitive damages if you believe Hypercom acted with a willful disregard for Lisa's rights.

"In our discrimination case we showed you that Philippe admitted he was treating her differently. We showed you there was no credible HR response. Doug Reich's testimony, oh, my Lord, was that filled with holes. How dismissive can you be? It's just that her claim was a bunch of junk, so we didn't have to pay attention to that. You're entitled to find that they had no effective policies and procedures in place to protect Lisa.

"As far as this retaliation, I mean, willful disregard of her rights. That's almost the exact point of our case. That's what we're here about. They intended

to hurt her. That's what they wanted. They knew about the lawsuit. They have no legitimate justification for it. It was the exact kind of spiteful act that allows you to give an award simply to make an example of their conduct.

"*I want to take a minute now to tell you why this case is important,*" Randy said as he began to wrap up his closing argument.

"*For the past four years the only thing she's wanted, the only thing she's asked for is for someone other than Philippe Tartavull and Doug Reich, someone other than that to be her judge and jury. And she got that, so thank you. Philippe created for Lisa a glass wall. Welcome to the club, but you're going to have to wait outside. You can look in. He put more walls up. Everyone gets job protection, severance, except you, another wall up. I will question you. I will not timely pay your commissions. Everybody else, I will. Put another wall up. I will not respect you. I will have meetings without you. I will exclude you from important events. I will call you a junior managing director.*

"*Lisa ended up living in a glass cage. Then when she stood up for herself, when she dared to stand up for herself, she is given a message, stay in your place…we're big, strong, we'll get you. They sued her for no reason at all.*

"*A jury can say to a powerful corporation and their army of lawyers, no, you don't have the right to ruin a life, tarnish a career just because someone tries to stand up for themselves. You don't have that right.*

"*Every time a woman like Lisa stands up for her rights, it makes it that much easier for the next superstar to get into that board room to make a difference without having another Philippe Tartavull ruin her, leave her for the scrap heap.*

"*You have the ability today just by following the law, just by following the law to send a powerful message in the United States of America, we the people, we are the culture of accountability.*

"*Please return your verdict in favor of Lisa Shipley.*"

Somberly, stoically, but firmly, Randy lifted up the pink highlighter and stood it on its end, leaving it on the podium as a visual reminder for the jury of all the untruths and misrepresentations that had been made by the defense. Then he calmly walked to the prosecution's table to retake his seat.

I sat speechless. Randy was incredible; I was so proud of him. I could almost feel a victory and I believed I could see it in the eyes of the jury. I looked over at good ole Charlie and to me he appeared somewhat shaken. "Follow that," I thought in my head. "Just follow that, Charlie."

- 19 -

HIGHLIGHTING
THE TRUTH

N ow it was time for the defense to present their final plea. Charlie began by trying to reinforce Hypercom's position that I had not been discriminated against, that I merely didn't like change.

"Lisa Shipley didn't like Philippe Tartavull. She didn't like the changes that he brought to Hypercom," Charlie began. *"She didn't like his management style. You've seen that in her own emails. But the fact that she didn't like him doesn't mean that he discriminated against her because she was a woman."* Charlie then belabored the fact that I never reported discrimination to human resources, nor did O.B. Rawls.

"Now the reason why Ms. Shipley never told Mr. Rawls or anyone else that Mr. Tartavull was discriminating against her, because it never happened. She didn't have to use the magic words, as Mr. Grayson said, but her complaints can't be about management style or the president being too tough on her or her team or ignoring North America or changing the culture of the company. It has to be some form of, he's treating me badly because I'm a woman."

Charlie then referenced board member Dan Diethelm's testimony. *"She came to him during that time when they were searching for a new CEO and said to him, if you make Mr. Tartavull the CEO I'm going to quit. She could have said he's discriminating against me because I'm a woman. He's treating me unfairly because I'm a woman. She said none of those things."*

He then tried to emphasize his statement about my not liking Philippe. *"What do Ms. Shipley's emails show about her and the way she viewed Mr. Tartavull? She made fun of his accent. She was purposely uncooperative.*

"In addition—you heard her say that he wouldn't deal with her, that he only dealt with her by email, that he wouldn't communicate with her, what does she say here, April 25th, 2007, to Mr. Rawls in this email? You send it—this answer that Mr. Tartavull is looking for, you send it. I want to get out of dealing directly with him. I report to you. So it was Ms. Shipley that did not want contact with Mr. Tartavull. It's an important email because Ms. Shipley testified that Mr. Tartavull wouldn't strategize with her, wouldn't help her, what she said that she wanted and needed. But what this email shows, and this email doesn't lie, she did not want to deal with him."

Charlie addressed the issue of my delayed compensation plan and claimed that the delay was actually O.B. Rawls' fault more than Philippe's. *"This delay in large part for the most was Mr. Rawls' fault. As shown in the email—she says on February 13, 2007, that's when Mr. Rawls sent her the proposed plan. She responds the next day with comments. He sits on it for the next six weeks until March 30th and when he says, will you please resend the comments to me? Then she's promoted on April 1st, and now Mr. Tartavull's involved. And it's Mr. Tartavull who then on April 29th says—apologizes to her for not getting to it. And her plan was approved three weeks later when she signs off."*

Charlie then tells the jury that I am confused about an employment contract and a severance benefit. *"Now Mr. Tartavull knew the difference, and this is defendant's exhibit 68, because Ms. Shipley's asking for an employment contract and severance increase. And he explains that to get an employment contract in the United States, that's for the very top executives in a corporation, but he says severance is another subject. And you heard from him that he was willing to consider that in 2008. And, moreover, he was willing to consider that in 2008 as part of a promotion for her to be the director, not just the managing director, not just for North America, but for all the Americas.*

"Despite the fact that Mr. Grayson said repeated times that Mr. Tartavull was a liar, how do we know that Mr. Tartavull was being truthful? Well, who did he hire for that position in 2008? He hired a woman, Heidi Goff.

"He hired a woman, Heidi Goff, for that very position. She replaced Ms. Shipley and then she was put in the job that he wanted to put Ms. Shipley in, managing director for all the Americas, not just North America, but South America and Central America as well. And Ms. Goff had a severance benefit in her offer letter. She was entitled to it under certain circumstances. Now, I would also note, finally there's no economic value to Ms. Shipley for a severance benefit because it's undisputed she resigned voluntarily. She wasn't terminated without cause. She wasn't there when there was a change in control, that is, the company being sold. So she wouldn't have been entitled to any money anyway if she had, quote, a severance agreement in place when she left on January 3rd."

|| ||| ||| ||

"Now you've seen evidence that compares her plan and her compensation to the other Hypercom managing directors. You know, was she was paid in a non-discriminatory way? Did she get equal pay for equal work? These are claims that you are going to decide when you deliberate. First, there was a difference between her managing director position in North America and the others. Now Mr. Reich talked to you about additional duties. And that's one of the things that you're going to have to find when you talk about her Equal Pay Act claim as you will see from your verdict form.

"Her job, even though it had the same title, is not the same because the managing directors outside North America didn't have the benefit of the corporate department to handle all the functions that you see in defendant's exhibit 101. So with these differences, the pay of all the managing directors outside North America was roughly comparable to Ms. Shipley's. And, although Mr. Grayson used this pink marker to cross out all these numbers on defendant's

exhibit 102, as you heard from Mr. Jones, at the end of the year, in the beginning of the following year there's always a little give and take and it's difficult to separate out exactly what was made in each year."

Well, if that wasn't—to use Randy's earlier term—a lot of hogwash. But, Charlie was sticking to his story. Charlie even had a good excuse for why it seemed that Philippe had treated me differently in meetings.

"At these meetings the people from North America didn't have the data that Mr. Tartavull was looking for. It has nothing to do with Ms. Shipley being a woman. It has to do with the fact that they didn't have the ability to generate the information. Again, this has nothing to do with discrimination. And you heard from Mr. Jones. He said Mr. Tartavull was tough on people who didn't know their numbers and Ms. Shipley is not a numbers person. So Mr. Tartavull was critical of the employees in North America in charge of sales for business reasons. He wasn't critical of Ms. Shipley because she was a woman."

When it came to an explanation for my not getting paid commissions on the sales I had generated during my last quarter before leaving, Charlie made that part rather short and to the point from Hypercom's perspective. *"As you heard from Mr. Jones, the policy is that the employee must be there when the revenue is recognized in order to get commission. That is when the sale is final."*

Charlie moved quickly to my claim that Philippe would not visit my customers. *"You heard from him* [Philippe] *that he had met with Heartland, Sonic, First Data and Key Corp, and was willing to meet with others. And, he's told you, toward the end of the year there's many other things going on, so there wasn't time for visits toward the end of the year. But there is absolutely no evidence that he ever refused to visit Ms. Shipley's customers."*

When Charlie moved to the subject of my claim of retaliation regarding Hypercom's lawsuit against me personally, he provided a clouded picture of legalistic information to try to convince the jury that they should deny my claim of retaliation.

"I want to start with the timing of those lawsuits and how they relate to other events in this case. So on June 26th, Ms. Shipley files her discrimination

charge with the EEOC, which, of course, she has every legal right to do. And she follows that up with a lawsuit on January 30th, the same. Now on August 30th, 2009, Mr. Boardman and Mr. Frey resign from Hypercom to join Ingenico. Okay. So from the time of June 26th, until August 10th, 2009, is 14 months. So what they want you to believe, what the plaintiff wants you to believe here is that 14 months later Hypercom suddenly decided to punish Ms. Shipley for filing her EEOC charge.

"And I want you to listen to the judge's instruction to you on the law with regard to this claim of retaliation. Because he's going to tell you that if you find that Hypercom's decision to sue the people in the company that they did sue was based on an action taken by Ms. Shipley after she filed the EEOC charge and the lawsuit, that's called an intervening action and it breaks the chain of events and there's no retaliation. So what was this intervening action? Well, what it was, was she admitted on the stand it was her recruitment of Mr. Boardman and Mr. Frey to Ingenico. That is precisely the intervening action that caused Hypercom to act. Had she not recruited Mr. Boardman and Mr. Frey away from Hypercom, there would have been no lawsuit. The necessary connection between the EEOC charge and Hypercom's lawsuits is simply not present, and because it's not present you must find for Hypercom on this retaliation claim.

"Now, I'm going to talk to you about damages now even though we believe that the evidence shows that Ms. Shipley shouldn't prevail on any of her claims and, therefore, is entitled to no damages. But if I don't talk about damages, Mr. Grayson is going to get up and say that I didn't say anything about damages, so whatever he says should control, so I am going to talk about it.

"I will agree with Mr. Grayson on one point, these damages cannot be quantified. Even the numbers where we're talking about lost pay or commission that she allegedly didn't get, they really can't be quantified and they haven't quantified them for you. And they have to prove those damages to a reasonable certainty, and the judge is going to charge you as to that, but they have not done so.

"In addition, the category of damages—compensating Ms. Shipley for emotional distress or pain and suffering, whatever the language the judge is going to use in his jury instructions to you, as you heard her, she never saw

a medical doctor. [He totally ignored my going to Care Now for heart palpitations.] *She never saw any kind of mental health professional whether psychiatrist, psychologist, or therapist. But if you do find for Ms. Shipley on any count—and again, I would say to you the evidence does not support doing that—but if you do that, the judge is going to give you an instruction that you are allowed to award damages of $1. And if you do find for her in any court, that is what I would urge you to do, damages of $1 because she hasn't proved any damages to a reasonable certainty.*

"*With regard to the idea that this is a case that's appropriate for Hypercom to be punished and to set an example for the rest of the corporate community in America and the rest of America, there's absolutely no support for that.*

"*There's absolutely no evidence of any type that Hypercom was either malicious or acted in reckless disregard of Ms. Shipley's rights.*"

|||||||||||

"*There's an old saying, which is, you don't leave your common sense behind when you go into the jury room. And your common sense here tells you that Ms. Shipley had a nice comfortable situation at Hypercom, but the board of directors was unhappy with Hypercom's performance. They were in a distant third place, as you've heard, in basically a three-company industry, so they appointed Mr. Tartavull the president and told him to improve Hypercom's performance. Mr. Tartavull came in with the goal, as you've heard, of changing Hypercom from a culture of entitlement to a culture of performance and accountability, and he did that, but Ms. Shipley did not react well to it. She told Dan Diethelm in the summer or fall of 2007 that, if you make him the chief executive officer, I'm going to leave. They did it, the board did it, and she left. She said nothing about any sort of discrimination to Mr. Diethelm even though that would have been her opportunity to do so and it would have meant that Mr. Tartavull would not have been the CEO.*

"*So what are we left with here at the end of our week together? We are left with Ms. Shipley's own words, and I've shown you some of them here and you've seen a lot of them throughout the week. And her own words are her undoing. Here is Ms. Shipley on July 16th, 2007, right after the reorganization was announced and Mr. Keiper was leaving and Mr. Tartavull was appointed the chief operating officer. She says, 'Damn, I wish I could resign and still get paid.'"* [This comment was clarified in earlier testimony as a comment made in an email by Lisa in reference to a newspaper article about Mr. Keiper's severance pay when he was relieved of his CEO position.]

"I thank you for your service, and I ask you to return a verdict for Hypercom on every question on the verdict form."

||||||||||

Randy was allowed to provide a rebuttal after Charlie's closing argument. He took full advantage.

First he addressed the issue of exhibits, admitting that he hadn't spent a lot of time going through them, but knowing that the jury would have all of them. *"You're going to be able to look through them. I can go through these one by one, but you paid attention this week. I know you did. We saw you pay attention. You will be able to read them. You will be able to figure it out.*

"Now, I just want to address a couple of things. This case from Hypercom's perspective is all about just telling you something and hoping it sticks. Hypercom just says, you know, there's a difference between an employment contract and a severance agreement, like, there's some sort of magic that Lisa, a salesperson, is supposed to know these technical terms are so different. You heard the general counsel say, what's a contract; contracts happen all the time. There's no term in the law out there that says an employment contract equals one thing and a severance agreement equals another. They just want to fool you.

"You heard from Dan Diethelm, you know, he comes in at the last minute, somebody we've never heard from before [there was no deposition from him on either side], *talks about a meeting in July that Lisa says never happened. She does remember talking to him in December. Who are you going to believe? And that's a very important point. It's a very important point. Because one*

thing Mr. Wayne said I think is very valuable and something you should take with you to the jury room. If you doubt the truthfulness of somebody's testimony, if you doubt their credibility, you're entitled to reject all of their testimony. Do you believe that Doug Reich was telling you the truth when he told you that severance agreements were determined by the law or the state or the countries? Do you believe that Clint Jones was telling you the truth when he tried to compare any of those compensation numbers to you? Do you believe you can believe Philippe Tartavull was telling you the truth when he told you that he was going to promote Lisa Shipley? Do you believe that? That's your job."

||||||||||

"And, here we are, here we are at the close. Did you hear it? Did you hear it yet? Have you heard a single reason why—why Hypercom calls Lisa a thief? Have you heard it yet? You haven't. They have no justification. They want to distract you. They want to tell you that Greg Boardman had a non-solicit agreement, therefore we should call Lisa a thief. Bernie Frey was in sales, therefore we should call Lisa a thief.

"You're going to get the jury verdict form and you're going to get a right to determine damages and you are going to get an instruction about the nominal damages of $1. And in every case you're also going to be able to consider both the monetary damages that were proved to you and the compensatory damages that you're entitled to award and the punitive damages that you're entitled to award. That's your job. I'm so honored to have been involved in a case where we get to stand up, where we get to stand up for the rights of people like Lisa, where companies can't just come in with rehearsed lines, just go through something they've prepared in advance, and we get the opportunity to show you that it's all a pack of lies.

"It's all a pack of lies. We get the opportunity to protect someone who stood up for herself, someone who said to you—which I think is the theme of this case—I'm glad I stood up for my rights.

"We trust you."

I was so pleased when Randy finally called it what it was, telling the jury, "It's all a pack of lies." I felt like the jury felt good about his saying that, too. No more niceness; just call it what it is. And, when he said, "We trust you," I thought to myself,—That's a perfect ending—I couldn't ask for anything more; we all did our best, we fought the best battle we could. Now the wait began.

In my heart, I felt cautiously optimistic. I was also a nervous wreck.

- 20 -

THE VERDICT

After nearly four years and a whole week of testimony, my day of reckoning had come. My emotions were mixed. I was excited and felt that Randy's closing arguments had left a clear picture of the wrongs I had endured from Hypercom and left the jury with a positive feeling about our case. I also was nervous, realizing that once the jury got behind closed doors anything could happen. I just wanted it all to be over, and until it was, my heart would keep racing and my mind would keep replaying all the things that had been said over the past week.

The judge called the jury back to the courtroom and advised them of the law before putting the deliberations and the verdict in their hands. He went on to explain the responsibilities of each party to prove their respective side of the case and elaborated on the specifics of my claim.

"In order for the plaintiff to prevail on her claim, she must prove the following by a preponderance of the evidence," the judge said.

"First: That she is a member of a protected class;

"Second: That she was subjected to an adverse employment action;

"*Third: That the defendant treated similarly situated male employees more favorably; and*

"*Fourth: That she was qualified to do the job.*"

He then elaborated a bit on a couple of the points, explaining, "*It is not necessary for the plaintiff to prove that her gender was the sole or exclusive reason for the defendant's employment decisions. It is sufficient if the plaintiff proves that gender was a determinative consideration that made a difference in the defendant's decision.*"

He explained the legal definition of gender discrimination and also explained the guidelines for determining a claim of unlawful retaliation. He elaborated on what the law allows and doesn't allow regarding the awarding of damages.

He then instructed, "*Any verdict you reach in the jury room must be unanimous. In other words, to return a verdict you must all agree. Your deliberation will be secret. You will never have to explain your verdict to anyone. Each of you must decide the case for yourself, but only after full consideration of the evidence with the other members of the jury.*

"*When you go to the jury room you should first select one of your members to act as your foreperson. The foreperson will preside over your deliberations and will speak for you in court.*

"*I've prepared a special verdict form that you will use in recording your decision. The special verdict form is made up of questions concerning the important issues in this case. You will take the verdict form to the jury room and when you have reached unanimous agreement you will have the foreperson fill in the verdict form, date, and sign it and then return it to the courtroom.*"

The verdict form had questions related to each of the counts, such as the following: Not providing severance benefits? Not attending the Cartes trade show? There was a box next to each question to mark yes or no indicating whether they found the defendant guilty or not, and a blank to fill in if they decided to award a dollar amount.

The judge then said, "*If you desire to communicate with me at any time, please write down your message and question and pass the note to the courtroom security officer who will bring it to my attention. I'll then respond as promptly as possible either in writing or by having you return to the courtroom so that I can address you orally."*

After further advising them that they may not use any electronic device or media such as a telephone or cell phone, he said, *"Members of the jury, you are excused to the jury room to select your foreperson. We will bring in the exhibits and the verdict form to you. And you may be excused at this time."*

Once the jury left, the judge addressed the lawyers and asked them how late they wanted to wait. Both sides agreed that they were there as long as the jury would like to be. *"All right. I'll let you know,"* the judge said. *"We'll be in recess."*

With that we left the courtroom and headed up the street to find somewhere to eat lunch. By now the courthouse cafeteria had closed for the day. Although I should have been hungry, the thought of eating made me feel sick; my stomach was tied in knots and my heart was racing so fast that I felt like I was in a fog. I wanted to talk—about everything. Most of all I wanted to hear some reassurance from my legal team that they thought we had done well and had probably won this case. As we walked we began to talk. Although there were those moments of discussion where everyone thought we had hit a home run, the bottom line from my lawyers was that I simply needed to prepare myself for anything. You never know what a jury will do, they told me.

We had just made it to the CNN Center where there are lots of shops and restaurants, when David's phone rang. The jury had a question; we needed to return to the court to hear their request.

What did this mean? What question could they have already? We had no clue what this could mean, but whatever it was, we needed to hurry back to the courtroom. We literally ran back and waited for the judge to enter.

What was it the jury wanted to know?

"Can we have a calculator?" was their request.

You're kidding, right? Neither side objected, but we looked at each other and all but jumped out of our chairs. Once we were dismissed and headed back down the street we started giving one another high fives, convinced that their request could only mean good things. Certainly, it meant that they needed a calculator to figure out how much they were going to award me. Or not. Maybe it meant that the numbers were so complex on the comp plan that they were running their own calculations? And, there were several other areas that they might have wanted a calculator to run numbers for. All that excitement came to a screeching halt and, at least for me, worry took over again.

It had been about 2 p.m. when the jury left to deliberate. One by one the hours passed with no word from the court. Was the long wait a good sign? Or was it a bad sign? We all tried to comfort each other, telling ourselves that the long deliberation must mean things were positive for us. But who really knew? Then finally about 6 p.m. we got the call—the jury had a verdict. At least we didn't have to wait until the morning.

|| | | | | | | | |

This was it. Each side had already started boxing up their mountains of paper, piling them in boxes. Waves of queasiness rushed through my stomach. Finally the jury came in. As they looked toward me I tried to read their faces. My gut told me they had found in my favor, but I couldn't be sure.

The courtroom was eerily silent; you could hear a pin drop. The verdict was handed to the judge and as he reviewed it in detail it felt like a half-hour was passing. Finally the judge began to speak.

"In the case of Lisa Shipley versus Hypercom Corporation, Civil Action Number 1:09-CV-265, we the jury, hereby find as follows: Paragraph one, do you find that plaintiff Lisa Shipley has proven by a preponderance of the evidence that defendant Hypercom Corporation intentionally discriminated against her in the compensation terms, conditions and privileges of her employment because she is a woman with regard to:

"The amount of her compensation?" Answer: *Yes. And we award plaintiff damages of $150,000.*

It was only the first charge, but upon hearing "yes" the tears began to pour down my face. I made no sound; just streams of tears.

"Delay in paying her commissions between September 1, 2007, and January 3, 2008?" Answer: *"Yes. And we award the plaintiff damages of $1,000."*

"Treatment at meetings?" Answer: *"Yes. And we award plaintiff damages of $7,000."*

"Not attending the Cartes trade show?" Answer: *"Yes. And we award plaintiff damages of $6,000."*

"Not visiting her clients?" Answer: *"Yes. And we award plaintiff damages of $10,000.*

"Not providing a severance benefit?" Answer. *"Yes. And we award plaintiff damages of $50,000."*

"If you found for plaintiff in paragraph one and awarded her damages, do you find by a preponderance of the evidence that defendant acted with malice or reckless indifference to plaintiff's right to be free from intentional discrimination based on her gender?" Answer. *"Yes. And we find that punitive damages should be assessed against the defendant in the amount of $500,000."*

"Paragraph three, do you find that plaintiff Lisa Shipley has proven by a preponderance of the evidence that defendant Hypercom Corporation retaliated against her for exercising her right to oppose an unlawful employment practice by filing the lawsuit against her implicating her in the lawsuits filed against Boardman, Ingenico and Frey? Answer: *"Yes. And we award plaintiff damages of $100,000."*

"Paragraph four, if you found for plaintiff in paragraph three and awarded her damages, do you find by a preponderance of the evidence that defendant acted with malice or reckless indifference to plaintiff's right to oppose an unlawful employment practice?" Answer: *"Yes. And we find that punitive damages should be assessed against the defendant in the amount of $500,000.*

"Paragraph five, as to plaintiff Lisa Shipley's claim under the Equal Pay Act, the defendant Hypercom Corporation paid her a lower wage due to her gender? Answer the following questions:

"Was Lisa Shipley and a male employed by Hypercom Corporation in jobs requiring substantially equal skill, effort and responsibility?" Answer: *"Yes."*

"Was Lisa Shipley paid a lower wage than a male performing equal work and under similar working conditions?" Answer: *"Yes."*

"Was the difference in pay between the two jobs the result of factors unrelated to Lisa Shipley's gender?" Answer: *"No."*

Jury: *"We find for the plaintiff with regard to her Equal Pay Act claim and award her damages for the difference in wages paid between the two jobs in the amount of $150,000."*

By now I was sobbing. The verdict was in and the jury had found for me on all ten counts—in total they had awarded me just shy of $1.5 million. I was in shock, stunned but relieved in the most powerful way possible. And most of all, I felt vindicated. This jury believed as I did that I had been discriminated against. That alone was a victory for me.

With tears streaming down my face I looked at each juror and silently mouthed, "Thank you."

|||||||||

The jurors left the courtroom while the rest of us stayed as the judge finalized things with the lawyers. About 20 minutes later we walked out of the courtroom. I couldn't believe my eyes.

There in the hallway stood every member of the jury. As incredible as it seems, every member of that jury waited outside the courtroom, not just so they could greet me, but so they could hug me. That's right. One by one each juror grabbed me and hugged me. They thanked me for letting them correct what they deemed a "clear injustice." They thanked me! I was overwhelmed.

They commented on the multitude of inaccuracies and out-and-out lies that many of the Hypercom witnesses had told and said it helped make their job easier. They also told me they loved Bernie—they said they knew he just could not bear being accused of lying.

It was a very emotional time for me, a very unexpected, emotionally supportive moment and one that I will cherish always.

For the first time in four long years I felt relief. We decided to celebrate our victory with dinner at my house. When I got in my car to drive home alone I simply sat there momentarily, emotionally overtaken by it all. I laid my face in my hands and just sobbed. But this time they were tears of joy. On the drive home I started making phone calls; I called my husband and I called my Chicago friend who I'd gone to in the very beginning, the man who had been so important in helping me stay in the fight when I felt I wanted to quit. I called my mom, Bernie, Greg—the list went on and on. All of a sudden my adrenaline was pumping full force! We had all won.

Back at my house we ordered in Chinese food, popped the champagne to decompress, and partied into the night. It was a great ending and a great win.

|| || || || || ||

As incredible as the outcome was, in some ways my victory was short-lived. The very day they could, Hypercom filed an appeal. I ultimately settled for far less money than the jury originally awarded me. Despite everything, I always said this suit was never about the money—it was about making it to the finish line and being vindicated by a jury of my peers. And for that to have happened I am forever grateful.

Would I do it again? No. Even though I ultimately "won," I'm not sure the emotional wear and tear on my family and me is something I could go through again. Unfortunately, organizations know this, and I feel it's one of the reasons discrimination cases like mine never go anywhere.

The statistics show that this kind of discrimination still exists but rarely does it get to court, let alone end up with a trial like mine. I believe these kinds of laws are continually broken in corporate America because the system favors big corporations with deep pockets. We need an overhaul or this type of discrimination—or frankly any kind of discrimination— will go on forever. My Chicago lawyer, David Ritter, summed it up perfectly when interviewed about the case. "They made Lisa fight and scrape and crawl on hands and knees across glass to win this case. They tried everything they could to win this claim, to demean her, to bankrupt her. And she prevailed because she was right."

It's time to break down the glass walls and make the system right.

– EPILOGUE –

IT WAS NEVER
ABOUT THE MONEY

Winning this case was never about money. The validation that a jury of my peers—men and woman who like me work for a living—let me know with their verdict is that I had been right to stand up for myself, and that I had, indeed, been discriminated against and they understood the emotional pain and distress I had endured because of it. Yet, there was also a financial cost to get there. Thus, the awards attached to each count were the jury's way of compensating me in the only way they could.

Even though the jury found Hypercom guilty, the legal system allows the defendant the right to file an appeal. And that's exactly what Hypercom (VeriFone) did. That, of course, delayed the payment of any part of the award. Then I found out that even though the jury had awarded me nearly $1.5 million, the state of Georgia had caps on what could be awarded to me—something I had never been advised of. As you can imagine, this was a shock. The bottom line was that even though I had filed two separate lawsuits against Hypercom—the gender discrimination suit and then two years later the added retaliation suit—they both fell under the same cap, which was $300,000 in total. Just like that—nearly $1 million gone in one fell swoop. With the $150,000 in unpaid wages and the new total under the cap, the award was suddenly reduced by two-thirds to $450,000.

The judge, however, had the right to award another $150,000 if he thought the actions of Hypercom were "deliberate." Fortunately, he did, increasing the award total to $600,000. Then there were legal fees. Since we had won, Hypercom (VeriFone) had to pay the fees that the court agreed to be fair. Once all the lawyers' billing was in, the judge chose not to award them all their requested fees but did award them approximately $750,000. That meant Hypercom (VeriFone) was still on the hook for over $1 million.

Once the judge had given his final ruling on the attorneys' fees in May 2012, Hypercom (VeriFone) realized that if they went through with the appeal process they would still have to pay all the legal fees regardless of the outcome. It apparently changed their thinking and we got a call from their lawyers telling us that they wanted to settle. We came to an undisclosed agreement and in June 2012, six months after the final verdict, Hypercom's (VeriFone's) appeal was dismissed by the court.

I'd like to tell you that my lawyers got paid all of their money and that I took home the $600,000, but that was not the case. What I personally ended up with was the commission money I should have been paid and the money I personally paid to my lawyers in the beginning, nothing more—certainly nothing close to the $1.5 million award. However, as I said before, this was never about the money. It was always about making it to the finish line and having it verified that I didn't deserve to be treated the way I was. I had done that. I had stayed the course to the end and the jury substantiating that I had been wronged meant more to me than any amount of money.

|| | | | | | | | |

While nothing will ever erase the memories of this long, agonizing ordeal, I have found that life does go on. And, as time passes, confidence and happiness also return.

I've chosen to continue to pursue success by using the talents and strengths that I've been blessed with. Today I'm using those talents in my new role as EVP and Managing Director TNS (Transaction Network Services) Network Division. It's an environment where my talents are valued and I can achieve as I'm naturally inclined to do.

I still live in the suburbs of Atlanta and enjoy a great personal life with my husband O.B. and Rachael, Daniel, and Adam, my three kids whom my world revolves around. I'm blessed to have some absolutely wonderful friends—especially Bernie and Greg—who lived the whole ordeal with me.

And guess what? I haven't lost my sense of humor either. Just ask my Atlanta lawyer, Randy.

When the trial was over I presented him with a very appropriate gift. I ordered him a large box of bright pink highlighters and had them personally inscribed to read "Randall Grayson." And right below the phone number…"The Pink Highlighter of Falsehoods."

ACKNOWLEDGEMENTS

This book represents a journey on a road that led me to some incredible people who were there to support me, guide me, and carry me during the worst of times. I got my day in court, in part because of these people, and my hope is that together we achieved victory.

Randy: My Atlanta attorney who believed in me and my case enough to fight beside me for four years, unpaid. Your grace, wisdom, and drive to fight one of the biggest law firms in the country was incredible. I believed in you, the jury believed in you and at the end, even the judge took off his hat to you and your efforts. I am forever grateful.

David and Nineveh: My Chicago attorneys—your support of Randy, your ability to find case law to support my claims, and your amazing ability to tell my story to the jury was the best. Thank you for being the professionals that you are.

There were many people who testified on my behalf:

Bernie: You rocked the jury with your raw emotion and believability. I hope in some small way you got your own day in court that you so well deserved. I'm honored to call you my friend.

Greg: I know how these events changed your life. I'm also well aware of your amazing ability to overcome and thrive. We always believed that we would "win" because we were right. The good shall prevail and in the end, it did.

Chris J: You and Ingenico stood by my side. To me you were my "Sir William Wallace" coming to my rescue throughout all of this. You are true to your name in every way and a man to be admired for your heart and soul.

Jaime: You came to my defense all the way from Mexico and you helped me validate in my own mind (and the jury's) all the things I'd witnessed and believed happened.

Chris A: Thanks for being my friend and helping to paint the true picture of who I am, my work ethic, standards, and validating my credibility in every way.

Ed: You "wowed" the jury by your presence in that courtroom and you supported me in every way through this case. You will always be someone I look up to and admire.

Fred: There is no doubt in the world that I never would have seen my case go the distance without your faith and support. Everyone needs a "Fred" in their life. Thank you.

Judge and jury: Thank you for seeing through the "smoke and mirrors" of the defense and ruling in favor of the "Pink Highlighter."

O.B.: Through some of the worst of times and the best of times, you will always be my best friend and my love.

Daniel, Rachael, and Adam: You are my greatest accomplishments. Nothing makes me more proud than being your mother.

ABOUT THE AUTHOR

Lisa Shipley has an impressive career history. As one of nine children she worked her way through college. She married at age 27 and divorced several years later, leaving her the single mother of three-year-old twins and a one-year-old. Lisa was naturally motivated to do what it took to provide a comfortable life for her children.

A career that began in banking soon led to an opportunity to get in on the ground floor of the technological advancement of the payment transaction business, where Lisa discovered that she was a natural-born salesperson. Within two years she became the global company's number one salesperson, an achievement that eventually made her one of five global managing directors and the highest-ranking woman in a male-dominated industry. Her meteoric career came abruptly to an end when a new CEO demeaned and demoralized her in what eventually caused her to resign and became the basis for her filing a gender discrimination lawsuit. On her resignation from Hypercom, she joined Ingenico, a competitor, and then moved to First Data Corporation, a former client company serving the transaction world industry. After a nearly four-year court battle with Hypercom, a jury of Lisa's peers found the CEO and the company guilty on all ten counts and awarded Lisa a $1.5 million judgment.

Today, Lisa remains a leader in the payments industry. Lisa resides in Atlanta, Georgia, with her husband, O. B. Rawls, and her three children, Rachael, Daniel, and Adam.

9 780692 249703